T0065765

SPONSORSHIP PAGE

THIS BOOK IS SPONSORED BY

....

....

AS A GIFT TO

....

....

ON THIS DAY

....

'Each one must give as he has decided in his heart,
not reluctantly or under compulsion,
for God loves a cheerful giver.'
(2 Corinthians 9:7, ESV)

Building Healthy Relationships

ADOPTING MEASURES & APPROACHES TO ENSURE HEALTHY RELATIONSHIPS

EMMANUEL ATOE

WESTBOW
PRESS®
A DIVISION OF THOMAS NELSON
& ZONDERVAN

WestBow Press books may be ordered through booksellers or by contacting:

WestBow Press
A Division of Thomas Nelson & Zondervan
1663 Liberty Drive
Bloomington, IN 47403
www.westbowpress.com
844-714-3454

Unless otherwise indicated, all Scripture taken from the King James Version of the Bible.

Scripture quotations are from the ESV® Bible (The Holy Bible, English Standard Version®), Copyright © 2001 by Crossway, a publishing ministry of Good News Publishers. Used by permission. All rights reserved.

ISBN: 978-1-6642-8784-6 (sc)
ISBN: 978-1-6642-8785-3 (e)

Print information available on the last page.

WestBow Press rev. date: 01/17/2023

CONTENTS

DEDICATION

This book is dedicated to my family.

A special thanks go to my family.

Thank you for believing in me and inspiring me to success. Your kindness, gentleness, love, and the presence of God makes my life full of joy. The LORD blesses you and keep you; The LORD makes His face shine upon you and be gracious to you; The LORD lifts up His countenance upon you and give you peace, in Jesus' Name. Amen.

Always be full of joy in the Lord. I say it again—rejoice!

INTRODUCTION

Adopting Measures and Approaches to Ensure Healthy Relationship

Life is made up of relationship and what we do, how we do it, and what we represent determine our level of satisfaction and success in relationship. In the beginning of mankind, God formed relationship and created a healthy atmosphere for Adam and Eve to be supportive of one another, but unfortunately the couple's fulfilment as plan by God was hindered by human sinful nature. There are many forms of relationship; however, this writing will be focusing towards adopting measures and approaches that will promote healthy couple's relationship. Relationships are not without problems and conflicts because couples have different perceptions and they also react differently in addressing or confronting issues. Relationship issues are common in every home because of different exposure and lifestyles and even Christian's homes struggle with issues. Problems and conflicts do pose unhealthy relationship if they are neglected and not dealt with in God's way. It is God's principle that people respond to their differences in a Biblical way and use their disagreements to stimulate growth and develop their lives and maintain healthy relationship. The Key factor is the ability for the couple to live together in love.

To achieve a loving and caring relationship, the following biblical and psychological approach will be reviewed and discussed:

- Confession of love with evidence – Trust, Freedom and Boundaries,
- Recognizing and Celebrating of Achievement in the Relationship
- Forgiveness
- Repentance/Remorse
- Non-judgmental or non-shaming approach
- Solution to Conflicts
- Voiding Loneliness in Relationship – Adopting effective communication
- Supporting one another – Understanding your spouse weakness and assist
- Transparency in Relationship (Avoid too many secrets)
- Controlling Relationship
- Sex in Marriage
- Sharing of values/Responsibilities
- Restoration/Redemption
- Adoption of Prayer

The adoption of these factors in a healthy manner will result in a fulfilling relationship. One of the goals of this research is to help the readers tackle mistakes that are unhealthy for us to dwell in and resulting in unfulfilling relationship. Healings comes in our lives when we have the ability to recognize our mistakes and being remorseful about our sin and confess it to one another (James 5:16). When mistakes are identified, forgiveness of sin is necessary for conflicts to be resolved. Forgiveness is not just something or a tool to promote healthy relationship, but also God's requirement for us to have a meaningful relationship with him and others. Many secular therapists see forgiveness as logical and they do not often adopt the concept in therapy because they feel that it is an imposed choice on the clients and it is against their wills and may likely expose the victims to more danger in the case of a relationship with domestic violence or rape issues. The Christian counselors see the concept of forgiveness as Christian duty and obedient to God's Word and as a tool to create environment for healing.

Relationship works well when the people participate and share values and interest in the relationship and act as lifting agents for a weak and falling partner (Galatians 6:1-2). It's helpful for couple in marriage to confront one another sometimes, but it should be with love because Non-judgmental or non-shaming approach creates atmosphere of reconciliation in the relationship.

Each of these approaches and measures will be captioned in a separate chapter and discuss in relation to biblical and psychological viewpoints.

ONE

Confession of love with evidence – Love or Affection, Trust, Boundaries and Freedom

Recognising the importance of a fulfilling relationship and the adoption of certain factors in a healthy manner are integral to our wellbeing. Life is made up of relationship and our wellbeing can impact on how we connect with others and having a good relationship gives us a purpose and sense of belonging. The quality of our relationship matters to every individual who desire happiness. Our affection, trust, boundaries and freedom will determine our level of satisfaction and success in relationship. Every individual wants to feel loved and connected to their partner. Love makes couples more positive and happier with a strong desire to move forward and find solutions together to issues. Affection is like medicine and can have a great impact on our good mental health. In 1938, Harvard University began following 724 participants as part of the longest-running study on human development in history. The study was developed to determine what makes us happy. The study explored every part of who we are, from physical and psychological traits to social life and IQ, to learn how we can flourish. Findings from the study were published in the 2012 book "Triumphs of Experience, with key results showing that happiness and health aren't of wealth, fame or working hard, but come from our relationships.

Emmanuel Atoe

A healthy human love is also the expression of that love in the form of affection and also a genuine interest, in various forms, ways and sincere actions like kisses, comforting touch or simple physical gestures of affection hugs, which definitely does more to the human soul to keeping each person feeling comforted, healthy, loved and secure within any kind of relationship. It is the responsibility of each partners to feel comfortable within a relationship, with the how to match up their desire, identifying the what, when and how much of physical affection. Physical intimacy is beyond basic love. A lot more than love, because it is a demonstration of the desire and confirmation that you are deeply fond of each other and truly interested in one another, and that you are together even within and without the early days, so called 'physical infatuation. According to the book "High Definition Life," the highest calling of a spouse is the call to love, just as it is the highest calling of our faith; loving God and each other. We all want to be loved. We long for someone to care for us from the heart, to cherish us and delight in our company. But many of us struggle to find true love because we confuse it with something else. No one who wants true love has to settle for mere sex. Sex is fun and enticing but it can't substitute for love (Palau, 2005, 46, 48-49).[1] Why not go after the real thing? Don't be content with less than value what you want to give! True love, the kind Jesus Christ offers to help you find, surpasses the sexual delights of sex at least five ways: Sex is goal to orgasm while love is intimacy; sex values performance while love values person; sex emphasizes looks while love emphasizes character, sex desires to get while love desires to give and sex means to an end while love end itself.

Couples who are truly relate to each other emotionally are those who feel loved, and feel accepted and valued by their partners. Love in a healthy relationship means being able to feel and understand your partner, as yourself. An individual who intimately understand and

---

[1] Palau, Luis, and Steve Halliday. *High Definition Life: Trading Lifes Good for Gods Best.* Revell, 2005. https://www.amazon.com/High-Definition-Life-Trading-Lifes/dp/0800718658

experience his [her partner], has the ability to feel what he [or she] feels, as much the way they also feel, able to know their thoughts, and to understand how they process what is happening to them becomes easier. The adaptation of love and intimacy is also demonstrated by showing how much we care and are completely comfortable to share all aspects of ourselves with our partners. Couples share mutual desire to open their soul to one another, because they love and cares enough about each other to understand and support one another fully in most everything they are doing. This kind of intimacy implies vulnerability, because to love makes an individual willing to show parts of themselves like weaknesses, fears, insecurities and the things they like least about themselves.

This adaptation of love makes an individual to feel safe and secured that the person he [or she] has chosen to have as a life partner knows him [or her] and accept him [or her], wants and all. Ruth Bell Graham on marriage wrote ["Where two people agree on everything" Our daughter's Swiss in-laws once gave my husband (Billy Graham) a Swiss watch. Eventually, it stopped working, and however hard we tried, we could not find a watchmaker that could repair it in the USA. Once visiting our in-law family, we asked them if they could get it repaired; being in Switzerland, they took it to the production factory, and there was no problem in getting it fixed quickly. It is still working to this day. I have thought about that; the watch, a complex mechanism, could only be repaired easily by those who "had created" it, and this is to us a parable of God's ways. The family, being a creation of God, can only be repaired by the Master watchmaker; every other effort will be in vain, as ours were to fix a man-made mechanism. Any human intromission into His mechanisms will not work, and will not repair the delicate balance of a hurt marriage: it depends on God that all things may work together for good to them that love His name, so that broken elements will be repaired…."] (Graham, 2010, 156)[2]. For a relationship to work well, each person has to understand their own and their partner's

---

[2] © Decision Magazine, July 2010

nonverbal cues. Knowing your partner deeply and providing comfort and understanding to someone you love is a pleasure, not a burden.

However, there is a fundamental factor that must be considered before this love can be strong and stable. That is the question of trust which can be considered, according to most people as undoubtedly one of the most important relationship characteristics, but I personally considered it as "the most fundamental relationship pillar." In the book by marriage ministries international, "married for life – "Life giving principles that make a marriage last", you will find this definitions of Trust: Strong's Concordance: ["to convince", "to rely (by inward certainty)", "yield", "obey persuade."; Dictionary: "reliance on integrity", "justice", etc.., "of a person, or on some quality or attribute of a thing"; "confidence"]. Trust is the thing regarded as reliably providing essential support for love to succeed. That is a solid foundation on which to build emotional intimacy (Phillips, 2000, 60)[3]. Love without trust is like a very beautiful expensive, latest model car without wheels, it goes nowhere, no matter how beautiful. So to build or run emotional intimacy, there must be mutual trust as a solid foundation on which to stand. The adaptation of commitment and trust are foundational to a healthy relationship. It must be emphasized that building these factors takes time and requires both partners to demonstrate through daily actions that they are dedicated to each other and the success of the relationship. Any individual who decides to embark on a romantic relationship, it is a necessary to encourage them to devote much effort and time and to enhancing their feelings of commitment and trust. Trust is our first essential task, according to Erickson's theory of the psychosocial stages of life, involves trust versus mistrust. It should be no surprise that our first goal in life is to master trust, since that is the basis for all of our relationships moving forward.

However it must be clarified that for many of us, our earliest experiences have been positive enough to allow us to adopt a trusting

---

[3] Mike Phillips, *Married for Life: Life-giving Principles That Make a Marriage Last: Leadership Manual* (Littleton, CO: Eden Pub., 2000), |PAGE|, p.60)

attitude. Some, though, have great difficulty with trust, perhaps as a result of certain past challenges or issues like inconsistency, invasion of boundaries, instability, or even actual threat of harm or alienation. This kind of mistrust must be dealt with properly, because it could lead to or manifest in isolation and avoidance of intimacy. It must be shared and communicated openly and honestly, so that the problem could be addressed properly together and if necessary get professional advice. In this case couples have to learn that an important part of love and intimacy is also the adaptation of a very good communication skill for a healthy relationship. When couples know what they desire from the relationship and feel comfortable expressing their needs, fears, expectations and mutually share or address the matters peacefully, it does increase trust and strengthen the bond between them.

In the case of Christians, I would like to illustrate this point further by making reference to the book "Marriage for Life", I quote "Faith and Trust" – ["Trust is only one way to staying in a marriage or rebuild a broken marriage. When trust in your spouse is broken you must place your trust in God. Forgive the sin and disappointment and trust God to change the circumstances. God is bigger than the problem and is able to change our heart. God never fails, and is working on that which concerns us and He will bring it to completion. Trusting God for change takes pressure off each other because trusting God to work in spouse frees him [or her] to grow. Trust is not based on performance and each spouse is even free to make mistakes knowing that God is bigger than the problem" (Phillips, 2000, 62)[4]

In the book Beyond Forgiveness by Don Baker, I quote "Every Christian have imperfections that requires encouragement, counsel, and kind admonitions and repentance We all have blemishes and weaknesses that tend to tarnish conduct and deportment but do not fall under the category of demanding severe discipline" (Baker, 1984,

---

[4] Mike Phillips, *Married for Life: Life-giving Principles That Make a Marriage Last: Leadership Manual* (Littleton, CO: Eden Pub., 2000), |PAGE|, p.62)

43).[5] To rebuild trust and love the individual that sinned, for example committed adultery, must take the responsibility by accepting his [or her] actions, repentance and the gravity of what was done. Recognize the pain and the betrayal that such action have caused the partner. In the case of a believer, it is a sin against God and against the partner, so true repentance to God and partner. Repenting does not mean that there will be no consequences for the sin, because an individual must deal with the results of his [or her] behaviour.

The individual must submit to counsel and talk with a pastor or spiritual leader, because the right way to solve the problem is to bring their heart into the open and become accountable and submitted to God and one another. As both partners seek to restore the marriage, there must be a willing to change for better. Trust can be lost in a moment, but it can only be gained over time so the couple must be patient and must not expect immediate results. It is natural for the hurt spouse to be suspicious or cautious for awhile. Trust can be restored, but it comes only as the spouse who sinned is open and honest and proved to be trustworthy. In relationship, most especially marriage there are many difficult situations that need counseling, but there is no situation or circumstances, no matter how complex or devastating that God could not handle, or where He withdrew His love.

Another adopting factor to keep a relationship healthy and secure is creating boundaries. Creating healthy boundaries is not self restriction but having shared and acceptable mutual freedom. Boundaries are not self imposed prison, they are not meant to make an individual feel trapped and it is definitely not a sign of secrecy type of relationship they both desire. There most be boundaries in every relationship and most especially for a successful marriage. Marriage break down when boundaries are not established in the beginning or the established boundaries are broken down. In marriage each spouse can act to avoid being a victim of the other spouse's problems and

---

[5] Baker, Don. *Beyond Forgiveness: the Healing Touch of Church Discipline*. Multnomah Press, 1984 (P43).

better still, to change the marriage relationship itself because God has designed each and everyone of us for freedom. Marriage is based on love relationship deeply rooted in freedom. However, I am not sugesting individuality, because just as couples have their "space" to spend time apart, it is equally very important that they spend time together. In my experince of counselling, I do suggest that couples spend time together but not "too much" time together, because it can create an unhealthy co-dependence. Therefore, for couples to stimulate and enrich their romantic relationship, it's important that couples sustain their own identity outside of the relationship, preserve connections with family and friends, and maintain their interests. So it very important that everyone is given the the necessary freedom to live their own personal life, most especially in certain areas like hobbies, profession, friendship, individual goals and aspirations,

It is important to set a boundary of how much time is appropriate together and apart. In this case the suggestion for a long and lasting relationship, is that there must be a balance of time spent together and apart, to enable a healthy autonomy and boundaries. Setting healthy boundaries are not meant to make you feel trapped; they are created to maintain respect and understand expectations in relationship, respecting each other and finding compromises to make the relationship work well. Therefore, boundaries need to be permeable, because love can only exist where freedom and responsibility are operating and boundaries are not something you "set on" another person, but yourself. This is self control. Research reveals that most authors and cousellors agree, that boundaries help define the freedom we have and the feedom we do not have or seek to have. Without clear boundaries it is difficult for spouses to know each other, and without knowing each other, they can not truly have freedom to love each other (Cloud & Townsend, 1999 46, 51).[6] However, an individual who does not respect his [or her] partners's need for time alone, but complains about not loved adequately or not receiving enough care because of less time together and actually makes him

---

[6] Cloud, Henry, and John Sims Townsend. *Boundaries in Marriage*. Zondervan, 1999.

[or her] feels guilty for time spent alone to recharge, most be given consideration, because every individual does not have the exact same needs in terms of alone time. There must be a mutual commitment, and a willingness to adapt and change with your partner.

In a strong, healthy relationship each individual has aspects of their lives that are personal, and that boundary is expected to be respected by both couples. The point, I am trying to emphasize is that there are many dynamics that go into producing and maintaining love, but the question of boundaries still remains one of the most fundamental issue. Boundaries are only built and established within the relationship. They are a set of personal limits that reinforce your sense of identity and autonomy. An individual have the ability to set them in order to protect himself [or herself] and demand respect. They will vary from relationship to relationship and can change over time. They can be physical, sexual, emotional and even spiritual. In a healthy relationship, communication about those needs leads to a workable compromise time altogether to strengthen both partners. The issue is trust or civil treatment because some amount of trust should be assumed or inherent within the relationship, when necessary for each individual to give their partner some independent and be able to dedicate time to cultivate their own personal interests.

TWO

Voiding Loneliness in Relationship –
Adopting effective communication

C ommunication is the sharing of information between different individuals. It includes the sharing of ideas, concepts, imaginations, behaviours and written content. It could simply be defined as the transfer of information from one place to another. Lack of communication in a relationship could cause serious problems. According to various experts in relationship, communicating honestly and respectfully, especially about issues that are difficult and probably unplesant, are not always very easy for an individual to share with other person, most especially a partner. As a matter of fact, most individual don't just automatically share honestly and respectfully their difficult issues or past events with their partners. This is not because they are dishonest, but simply because it does not come easy for individuals to discuss difficult matters with their partners.

In couseling, you discover that some individuals are not open with their partners on issues about their hopes, vision, aspiration, and even past events. There are various reasons individuals practice to keep uncomfortable things under the surface: first and foremost, most individuals have never been taught or able to learn how to acknowledge difficult feelings, while others probably for the inward false perfection or the appearance of perfection and most especially the majority simply keep something to themselves for the sake of what they call peace, traquility or harmony. This desire to maintain peace, at all cost could be a challenge to prevent a conflict or prevent an existing conflict from escalating into a full blown dispute. They don't discuss bad issues but instead "sweep issues under the rug." Whatever the reason, there is an issue of a lack or deficit of ability to personally talk or take things over. I define it, simply taking responsibility of one's action, to be honest and respectful even when an insividual's feelings are threatened. No matter how awkward or uncomfortable it feels, learning to share will make for a long lasting and fulfilling relationship. However, it must be clarified that not everyone knows how to communicate properly, some individual don't even communicate at all. Couples who mask their true selves, hide their emotional realities or actively deceive their partners about their habits and behaviours are jeopardizing the fundamental foundation of trust that every relationship needs. So couples should learn to communicate because disagreements are not necessarily a threat to a marital relationship an issue addressed in workshop and book "Seven Principles For Making Marriage Work" by Dr. John M Gottman. According to relationship researcher and the clinician, Gottman, disagreements are not necessarily a threat to a marital relationship. In fact, two thirds of disagreements are not resolvable, meaning that we learn to live with them and we make compromises. The problem is when we cease to communicate with our partner. We don't need to agree about everything to be kind to one another and to have a fulfilling relationship. Try to give your partner the benefit of the doubt and to understand where they're coming from. Clearly communicate your wants and needs. Recognize others are not mind readers. Nor are you. Do not assume (Gottman 1999).[7]

Happy and healthy relationship vocalize their love for one another, saying "I love you" often and offering compliments. In order to move forward and grow, couples need to be able to truly talk about their feelings. A healthy communication is not just one of the most important qualities of a healthy relationship, but the

---

[7] Seven-Principles-For-Making-Marriage-Work: https://www.gottman.com/product/the-seven-principles-for-making-marriage-work/#&gid=1&pid=2

lifeblood that nourishes good relationships, so individuals going through these tendencies (difficulties in communication), must make every effort to work on them personally, but if the situation continuous must seek help through couseling. In the book, by Dr John M. Gottman, According to him the advent of texting has only made things worse in relationship. I quote "A lot of couples refer to texting or email to discuss difficult things, If they have a fight, they text their apologies or defenses. If they are feeling distance, they text love notes. You lose so much communication through black and white words on the screen." In the hope of turning things around, this book guides new and noncommunicative couples through a series of themed dates, with accompanying, open-ended questions aimed at digging deeper and growing closer. "A tested program of eight fun, conversation-based dates that will result in a lifetime of understanding and commitment, whether a couple is newly in love or has been together for decades" (Gottman).[8]

Couples should start making the time and commit to listening to each other. Find the right words for how you're feeling and ask your partner questions about how they are (the book provides a list of options for both). Make exploratory statements, such as "Tell me what you're most concerned about" and express tolerance and empathy, which is as simple as saying, "I understand how you feel." Each chapter has conversation topics, preparation (read: homework, in the form of questions) and includes suggestions on where to have the dates, what to wear and what to bring ("An open mind and a willingness to be vulnerable with your partner," they write on the sex and intimacy date). "They are an invitation to dialogue, for couples to plunge deeper into themselves, their history and their experience, and to share that with an individual."

The good news is that good and healthy communication skills and the ability to tolerate a different point of view can be taught and learnt by couples who have the desire and will to grow in their relationship. The question of honesty and openness is not an open

---

[8] Gottma, John, Eight Dates: Essential Conversations for a Lifetime of Love

and close issue, because every individuals have different levels of openness within their relationships. There are couples who are able and willing to discuss the most intimate of physical details with each other without giving it a second thought, while some simply keep something to themselves for various reasons. There are individuals who don't listen and cannot observe their problems or conflict while there are other individuals who does listen and do communicate. The fact that everyone is open to feedback does not make an event of conflict communication an easy matter.

However, with regards to this issue, there are two kinds of people: those who listen to feedback called "boundary lovers" and those who don't listen to feedback and cannot observe their problems called "character disorder." The good news is one partner must see or notice the problem first and see it as a problem or conflict (Cloud &Townsend, 1999, 39).[9] Then honest talk with each other because you cannot solve a problem that you don't talk about. In a healthy relationship an individual must communicate the truth in love to enable the partner know what is wrong. The partner that is the problem should own it and confess, repent and apologize, while the partner who has been hurt, should communicate the hurt, accept the repentance, forgive and forget. Both should then commit to change. Conflict can be painful even if everyone is open to feedback. However, couples should not be afraid of conflict, but become boundary lovers and be open to truth, responsibility, freedom and love. This actually lead us to the next topic or chapter which is solution to conflicts. Finally, in a healthy relationship our stand should be I will hang in there with you because I care for you more than anything in the world. Our marriage is bigger than any issue. No matter who or what is arrayed against us, we will stand together. Neither of us will ever go through a trial alone.

---

[9] Cloud &Townsend, Boundaries in Marriage, 1999, (39).

THREE

Solution to Conflicts

A healthy conflict resolution is very essential in a healthy relation. According to various experts in relationship "Learning how to handle disagreements and work together to come up with a solution is one of the most important aspects of good partnership," I strongly believe it is crucial to have this ability because without it, you're potentially signing for a non happy and unhealthy relationship. The society will tolerate conflict in the beginning of romance but once a couple is involved in a serious relationship or married, they expect things to be different, that is "conflict free." However, in every relationship, there are arguments to be discussed, issues are brought to the forefront, and couples must be able to work through the hard times together to create a happy and healthy relationship.

In the book "Beyond Forgiveness: The Healing Touch of Church Discipline, By Don Baker, the church leadership just like any family had to take into consideration in chapter five "A search for Answers" finding the right solution to any problem without generating into a conflict. Every healthy family must take into consideration the importance of solution finding in a relationship. This is an extract from my perception of the chapter "The effect of Church disciplinary action towards Greg (pastor who sinned, committed adultery with different women). They were concern that applying some form of discipline may cause division and conflicts as Greg was a likable man. Hence scriptures were reviewed and used to enssure that church discipline is not just an option, but required (Baker, 1984, 33).[10] The scripture in Matthew 18:15-20, which indicates a sinning Christian is to be confronted, reproved, and excluded from the church if he refuses to change, was used to explain the need for church discipline.

The purposes of discipline in the church is to honour Christ by an act of obedience through the practice of discipline, to restore sinners. Therefore the aim of discipline is not exclusion but restoration and to discourage others from sinning. Confrontation, or the act of addressing the problem of sin in a brother's life, must be pre-prayed, pre-thought and pre-planned. This must be undertaking in a spirit of love and fear of God. The church is the spiritual family of God, so that in the church discipline should be confined to those "in Christ" and does not reach out beyond the boundaries of the church to the world."]

Research reveals that you can predict a lot about a couple's relationship's success from the way they are able to talk it through with love, kindness, gentleness, empathy, respect, and understanding, whenever there is an issue, problem, difficulties or difference of opinion without escalating into personal attacks or dispute. It also reveals that most couples that hide their upset with one another in order to preserve the illusion of everything being perfect, i.e. the so called "conflict free". Such individuals are probably far worse off than the couples that express their emotions and work to resolve them as they come up, even when it causes conflict. The scripture says in Matthew 7:12, "So in everything, do to others what you would have them do to you". There is no doubt that couples have a duty or responsibility to set limits on each spouse's or partner's destructive acts or attitudes. Although human nature tends itself to trying to change and fix others so that we can be more comfortable. We have no power over the attitudes and actions of other people. The law of power clarifies what we do and don't have power over.

In the book "Peace with God" by Billy Graham, from the chapter

---

[10] Baker, Don. *Beyond Forgiveness: the Healing Touch of Church Discipline.* Multnomah Press, 1984, (p33).

on "A Christian view of Marriage", I quote ["They (husband and wife) are to submit to each other – to love each other. Marriages entered into with a clear understanding of God's purpose and God's laws have no need for divorce courts. Marriages that fall short of this ideal (and it is appaling how many of them do) should first seek to learn what God expects of the husband and the wife, and pray for God's help and guidance in carrying out His commands." (Graham, 2017, 261)],[11] Couples who are Christians are called to love as Christ, knowing that the fruit of the Spirit is self-control not other control. We do not have the power to make our spouse into the person we would like him or her to be, but we don't have the power to be the person we would like to be, either.

Generally most people are very good at communicating warm, less important and easy things. But when it comes to working out the hard, difficult issues and differences of opinion, this lead to unpleasant fighting, because most couples don't have a clue as what to do. Couples that have adequate skills in this area are able to deal better with the situation, building a stronger relationship. In the book Billy Graham Speaks "insight from the world's greatest preacher" by Janet Lowe, (This book Billy Graham Speaks was created through the independent research of the author. It has not been authorized by it's subject). I would like to quote the following on Marriage [12]["many marriages end by the fifth year because couples haven't learned how to adjust. Differences can be settled amicably if both are really seeking the Lord's will ….. A man especially needs to learn to be extremely gentle. A woman must have tenderness from spouse; she no matter what he looks like or whether or not is successful. He have found that marriage should be made up of two forgivers. He need to learn to say, I was wrong ' I'm sorry. And we also need to say "That all right I love you."]

This law of sowing and reaping is evident in two areas of marriage, that is relationship and function. Most couples simply

[11] Graham, Billy. *Peace with God: the Secret of Happiness.* Billy Graham, 1984, (P261)
[12] Lowe, Janet. *Billy Graham Speaks: insight into the world's greatest preacher.* John Wiley, 1999 – ISBN 0 471345350

need counseling to learn how to travel together through the tunnel. The ability or willingness for couples to listen to each other's opinion or point of view is important. In a relationship, if an individual sow mistreatment of people, he or she reaps people's not wanting to be around him or her. There cannot be growth without learning that actions have consequences. If we are not acting out of revenge or desire to hurt, it is an act of love to allow our spouse to reap the effects, of his or her selfishness or irresponsibility. An individual that constantly interrupted, does not consider the opinions expressed by his [or her] partner, and such individual needs to learn how to resolve conflict. Another individual that quickly dismisses issue and never acknowledged the issue presented by the partner needs to work to resolve issues properly.

In reference to the article on "HUFFPOST" "Marriage Arguments: 10 ways to cope during a bad spot" by Dr Heitler for YourTango.com dated 05/07/2013, "In the situation where there's no chance to reason between married partners, then they have to consider that the time has come for them to choose a marriage and seek out quichly his [or her] help (Heitler, 2013).[13] Having a seasoned marital counsellor to help with the relationship should always be your last resort, but if an individual consider that he [or she] actually need to hire a counsellor, and put back on track the relationship with the partner, that is fine. However, loving each other better will certainly lead to a better life together, because it is normal to sometimes get into arguments, and to even have occasional intense debates with a partner, but no one should cross the admitted threshold. We all need to learn, to have fruitful and engaging arguments with our partners, take time to learn to debate, acknowledge the situation righteously, and have patience with them. We can get to know our partners better and have better and enriched lives together with them by learning how to cope with each other's issues." But, if we only focus on the negative side of things and only accuse and blame, this will only

---

[13] https://www.huffpost.com/entry/marriage-arguments_n_3225484

prove to cause more havoc in the relationship than is needed. This is definitely not the way to avoid conflicts successfully in marriages.

Another vital issue, is the conversation because it is very important that it must not be dominated by the outspoken partner, without taking into considerations the feelings of the other partner and worse still, not listening or taking account of the giving feedback. Individuals should take care to listen and know how their behaviour impacts their partner's feelings, instead of resulting to prompt dismisssl or shifting blame to make the partner feel that his [or her] opinion is not valid. Couples cannot expect any thing to happen, if they keep doing the same thing, they need to take action. They must give more considerations to change some choices, attitude, reaction and behaviour. Each partner must actively participate in the resolution of whatever relational problem they might have, even if an individual feels it is not his [or her] fault, because both parties have a responsibility to work hard at staying together in a healthy relationship. Responsibility shows us that we are the one who must work through our feelings and learn how to feel differently because our attitudes and not those of our partner causes us to feel distressed and powerless. True love in times of conflict is the product of deep trust between husband and wife. Trust says, "I will depend on you to guard and protect my heart and my life, to fight beside me always." You may need to trust a lot of people to pull you through a crisis. But more than anyone else on earth, husbands and wives should rely on each other. So during difficult moments or crisis which comes to every relationship, working together to come up with a solution is one of the most important aspects of good partnership.

FOUR

Forgiveness and Patience

T he fact of the matter is no matter who causes a problem, we are called to take steps to solve it. The scripture says in Matthew 5:9, "Blessed are the peace makers, for they shall be called the sons of God". Those who seek peace are the children of God. The first step is willing to forgive and be patience. Forgiveness and Patience are essential qualities for a healthy relationship. No one can be perfectly patient at all the times, and factors like lack of sleep, stress, or physical health problems will make an individual more easily agitated at various points in his [or her] life. The scripture says in [14]Proverbs 10:10, " ... People who wink at wrong cause trouble, but a bold reproof promotes peace. ... Those". So "whosoever winks malisciously causes grief, and and a chattering fool comes to ruin."

The fact that forgiven and patience are essential for a healthy and functional relationship is not a license for lack of responsibility. This issue most be addressed because sometimes dispute arises when the individual who has the problem or responsible for the issue isn't facing the effects of the problem. The spouse who is taking responsibility for the problem that is not

his [or hers], i.e the individual that forgives with patience must at a point in time, if the problem continues decide to say or do something about it, which helps place both the sowing and the reaping with the same person and begins to solve the boundaries violation. Patience

---

[14] https://biblehub.com/proverbs/10-10.htm

and forgiveness must be accompanied with boundaries. So in order to set limits in marriage, a proper view of responsibility is very essential. Forgiveness does not prevent accountability or give access to each spouse taken ownership for his or her mate's life or responsibility, because we are responsible to each other but not for each other. Spouses may help each other out with loads, but definitely each person must take care of his or her own daily responsibilities. We must deny ourselves certain freedom to say or do whatever we'd like in order to achieve a higher purpose. This enables us to take ownership of ourselves or simply said taking responsibility and this certainly removes limitations to our spiritual growth.

However, forgiving others is an absolute necessity for a healthy and successful relationship. As Christians, if you forgive an individual when they offend or hurt you, your Heavenly Father will also forgive you. But if you do not forgive, your Heavenly Father will not forgive you. The first step is to realize the absolute necessity of forgiving others. If we allow a spirit of unforgiveness to linger in our heart towards others, regardless of what they may have done against us, the scripture says in Luke 11:26, "Then it goes and takes seven other spirits more wicked than itself, and they go in and live there. And the final condition of that person is worse than the first." An individual opens his [or her] heart to enter in "seven other spirits more wicked than unforgiveness". These are progressively more degrading spirits, such as resentment, ill-will, grudges, malice, retaliation, bitterness and hatred.

The advice to couples during counseling is to refuse or resist to speak unkindly against an individual who have wronged you. Instead, show them kindness and godly love. The scripture say in Ephesians 4:32, "be kind one to another, tenderhearted, forgiving one another, even as God for Christ sake hath forgiven you". Believers know that we cannot do this by our own strength but through the power of God. We should allow the Holy Spirit within us to work through us, achieving God's grace and purpose in our life to show kindness, love, goodness and patience. Every Spirit-filled Christian has the fruit of the Spirit according to Galatians 5:22. The Holy Spirit in the life of a Christian will enable that individual to forgive all who have wronged him or her, even as God for Christ's sake has forgiven you. God's ability within a Christian is unlimited, so look, obey and yield to God for His supernatural ability, whereby, you can truly forgive others. Whether the individual who has offended you ever asks your forgiveness or not, you are required to forgive and to put all offenses under the blood of Jesus.

Some of the greatest problems we encounter in life are "people problems". We live in a world where communication can break down, where conflicts arise between friends, family members and couples, and where close ties may even be severed. We are faced with opposition and even misunderstanding. However, God has made a provision for every problem and has given us the ability to love with His love, to see others through eyes of tender love, mercy, grace, compassion, to forgive and better still forget about it. In the scripture Colossians 3:12-13, We are called to put on therefore, as the elect of God, holy and beloved, bowels of mercies, kindness, humbleness of mind, meekness, long-suffering; Forbearing one another, and forgiving one another, if any man have a querrel against any even as Christ Jesus forgave us, so also do we".

Forgive to be free is an aspect dealt with in the book "Your Best Life Now – 7 Steps To Living At Your Full Potential" by Joel Osteen. The story of Rudy Tomjanovich, the former coach of Houston Rockets basketball team. An event in 1973, at the age of twenty-five-years-old, while trying to break up a fight at the center court, he was forced to end his career because of a punch that fractured his skull, broke his nose and cheekbones and nearly killed him. Although he was sidlined for months following the devastating blow, he eventually recovered. Though it led to the end of his career, he tolda curious and disbelief reporter that has completely forgiven the player that did that to him, because he knew if he wanted to move on with his life, he had to let go. Rudy said, "I didn't do it for him, I did it for me. I did it so I could be free" (Osteen, 2015, 160-161).[15]

---

[15] Osteen, Joel. *Your Best Life Now: 7 Steps To Living At Your Full Potential.* Warner faith, 2017, (P160, & 161).

That's good advice. You need to forgive so you can be free. Forgive so you can be happy. Forgive so you can get out of that bondage. We have to remember, when we forgive we are not doing it just for the other person, we are doing it for our own good. When we hold on to unforgiveness and we live with grudges in our hearts, all we are doing is building walls of separation. We think we are protecting ourselves, but we are not. We simply shutting other people out of our lives. We become isolated, alone, waeped and imprisoned by our own bitterness. Those walls aren't keeping people out; those walls are keeping the individual in. An individual must forgive the person who hurt him [or her], so that he [or she] can move out of the prison. Get that bitterness out of your life. That's the only way you are going to truly be free. You will be amazed at what can happen in your life when you release all the poison. Forgiveness is a choice, but it is not an option. If you want happiness, freedom, joy and peace practise forgiveness.

I strongly suggest forgiveness to be practice by everyone, in respective of their religious beliefs or background, if they truly desire or wants a functional and healthy relationship and most especially desire a healthy and happy life. In forgiveness everyone comes out victorious, but the individual that forgives actually gain more than everyone else, because prevents, safe guard himself or herself the pain or hurt any time the memory brings back the offence to mind. The scars maybe there forever, but forgiveness prevents the pain or hurt from coming back again or being re-opend afresh. Forgiveness is a blessing in disguish to the individual that learns to practice or yield to it.

In the book "Beyond Forgiveness by Don Baker" Joanna (Minister's wife) experienced great anger, bitterness, and self pity and her contented past seemed to be more and more obscured with an ugly awareness that she had been deceived, betrayed, cheated and wronged. The past thirteen years spent with her husband Greg is blurred into one long nightmare because of his sin of immorality. She found herself turning even the most innocent events into ugly experiences but she never seriously considered leaving her husband because the real biblical option that she had was to forgive her husband (Baker, 1984, 73-76).[16] In order to achieve this aim, she look back on her childhood training in forgiveness with reference to the scripture in Ephesians 4:2 "Be completely humble and gentle; be patient, bearing with one another in love." Furthermore, she loved her husband Greg and had always spent large amounts of time together, so she resented being apart even when Greg would live home for one of his many conferences. They were a close family, love each other and Greg and Joanna never slept well unless they cuddle. Another problem Joanna had to face was that forgiveness did not guarantee her ability to forget, so she needed counselling to overcome deep feeling of guilt, periodic bouts with quiet anger and temporary desires to withdraw, even recoil from her husband.

Therefore, couples in a healthy, loving relationship are expected to demonstrate to one another compassion and patience that allows for flexibility, support and peace when a partner is having a bad moment or is passing through some difficult moments. Individuals that are always impatient with their partners, often create bitterness and resentment, when confronting the offense, that the other partner has committed. They live in constant resentment, ill-will, grudges, malice and maybe retaliation and bitterness instead of allowing unconditional love. I am in no way contemplating or suggesting that everyone can or must be be perfectly patience all the times, because circumstances like job situation, even traffic, stress or inadequate rest or sleep could lead to impatient. However, despite the challenges, I still strongly recommend patience and forgiveness, though we must also expect from a relationship some form of accountability because it is very easy or common for an individual to blame and focus on the mistakes of his or her partner. The will or ability to own our mistakes and errors, makes patience and forgiveness less stressful and creates a more successful and healthy relationships.

Finally four essential points to consider when we forgive: Love

---

[16] Baker, Don. *Beyond Forgiveness: the Healing Touch of Church Discipline*. Multnomah Press, 1984(P. 73-79).

covers (overlooks) a multitude of sins. The scripture says in 1 Peter 4:8 "Above all, love each other deeply, because love covers over a multitude of sins." Forgive a repentant, restore one who has sinned against us and reaffirm your love. The scripture says in 2 Corinthians 2:7-11 "so that on the contrary you should rather forgive and comfort him, otherwise such a one might be overwhelmed by excessive sorrow. Wherefore I urge you to reaffirm your love for him. For to this end also I wrote, so that I might put you to the test, whether you are obedient in all things. But one whom you forgive anything, I forgive also; for indeed what I have forgiven, if I have forgiven anything, I did it for your sakes in the presence of Christ, so that no advantage would be taken of us by Satan, for we are not ignorant of his schemes.; Restore with gentleness one who has fallen into sin. The scripture says in Galatians 6:1 "Brothers and sisters, if someone is caught in a sin, you who live by the Spirit should restore that person gently. But watch yourselves, or you also may be tempted.; and Love keeps no record of wrongs.

So if we desire to forgive and forget, we must do it by practice, counselling, help from the Holy Spirit and the grace of God. Everyone of us nust realize and accept the fact, that the act which offended or hurt us might always be with us, but forgiveness can lessen its grip on us and help free you from the control of the individual who harmed you. Forgiveness doesn't mean forgetting, making up with the person who caused the harm or excusing the harm done to an individual, absolutely this is not the case or finding of this research. An individual who has been hurt by the actions or words of his [or her] partner have wounds, with lasting feelings of anger, bitterness, that could lead to resentment. The practice of forgiveness and patience, in a relationship involves a decision to let go of anger, bitterness, resentment and thoughts of revenge, a decision that has great rewards of hope, gratitude, peace, and joy. It is the road that leads to unquestionable emotional, spiritual and physical well-being. Forgiveness and patience is one way to have peace of mind, less anxiety, less stress and hostility, fewer symptoms of depression, improved mental health, lower blood pressure, a stronger immune system, improved heart health, improved self-esteem, improved health and a healthier relationships.

In two books [17]"Marriage on the Rock" [18] "The Four Laws of Love" by Jimmy Evans helps couples learn how to succeed in marriage by applying these four laws to their relationship. Marriage offers that intimacy of body, soul and spirit, but only if we follow God's laws for marriage. One of those laws is the Law of Purity. True intimacy is only possible in an atmosphere of purity. For many marriages, unforgiveness is the sin that introduces impurity to the relationship. Maybe there's something in your spouse's life that you have not forgiven. A past hurt or offense may be affecting your ability to love each other as you should. That issue can be resolved with forgiveness. You won't know real intimacy in your marriage until you deal with it. The Bible says unforgiveness poisons our hearts. In marriage, unforgiveness is like a dead skunk in a basement: It makes the entire house stink. If you've ever been around unforgiving people, you've heard them speak venomous words about the people they resent. But you don't have to hear their words to know what's in their heart. You can see it on their faces and in their actions. The venom of unforgiveness damages the vessel it is stored in worse than it hurts anyone you can spit it on. In other words, when you do not forgive others, the person you hurt most is yourself. Unforgiveness doesn't just poison an individual's heart. It also poisons a marriage, even if the unforgiven offense isn't related to the relationship.

Moreover, harbouring resentment or bitterness toward others in your life will still have a negative effect on your marriage. In so many marriages, I've seen one spouse become the outlet for anger and frustration unrelated to the marriage relationship. If unforgiveness is poison, then forgiveness is a purifying agent. When we forgive others—especially a husband or wife - we get rid of unhealthy thoughts and feelings. Forgiveness cleans out the house.

---

[17] Evans, Jimmy. *Marriage on the Rock: Gods Design for Your Dream Marriage.* Majestic Media, 2012.

[18] Evans, Jimmy, and Craig Groeschel. *The Four Laws of Love: Guaranteed Success for Every Married Couple.* XO Publishing, 2019.

It blesses a relationship. It even impacts whether or not God forgives you. Forgiving other people is a serious issue with God and one of the requirements of a marriage that follows God's Law of Purity. There are five important steps to forgiveness: Release the guilty person from your judgment. Do not keep replaying the offense in your mind. Do not dwell on your hurt feelings or pain. Let God be the judge and let it go. Forgiveness is a decision. Make a decision to love the person who has offended you, then let your behaviour reflect that decision. In cases of abuse or destructive behavior, of course, you might have to limit your exposure to certain people. But your spirit toward them should be loving - not hostile. Pray for that person.

Jesus taught us to bless those who curse us and pray for those who mistreat us. This is one of the most powerful ways to change negative feelings toward a person. I've seen prayer transform deep resentment and hurt into love and compassion, - even without the presence of an apology. This is the most important step to take in healing the hurts of your past. Though it may take days or weeks, God uses this posture of prayer to heal us. By the way, the refusal to bless or pray for a person is proof-positive that you aren't forgiving toward them. Refuse to bring up the hurt in the future. When God forgives us, He removes our sins "as far as the east is from the west" He doesn't simply forgive; He forgets.

Though we cannot erase hurts from our memories, we can make the decision not to dwell on past offenses. This decision alone can have enormous positive impact on a marriage. Forgiveness is often a process, so repeat these steps as many times as necessary. Keep going through these steps until you sense a genuine release of the unforgiveness in your heart. A successful marriage is one-hundred percent possible if we follow God's laws for marriage. A marriage that obeys the Law of Purity must be one in which forgiveness is present. As you walk in forgiveness, you'll see a marked difference in the atmosphere and pleasure of your relationship. Purity is the environment where love and intimacy find their deepest and most beautiful expression. Forgive your spouse. Forgive those who hurt you. Be diligent to remain pure, and God will bless you beyond your wildest dreams.

Finally, this brings us to the next topic of research in the next chapter, that is forgiveness can even lead an individual to have towards the partner who hurt him [or her] feelings of compassion, understanding and empathy "understanding your spouse weakness and assist."

FIVE

Supporting one another –
Understanding your spouse
weakness and assist

T he holy scripture says in Galatians 6:1-5 "Brothers and sisters, if a person is discovered in some sin, you who are spiritual restore such a person in a spirit of gentleness. Pay close attention to yourselves, so that you are not tempted too. Carry one another's burdens, and in this way you will fulfill the law of Christ. For if anyone thinks he is something when he is nothing, he deceives himself. Let each one examine his own work. Then he can take pride in himself and not compare himself with someone else. For each one will carry his own load." According to the holy scripture, carrying one another's burdens, is the way an individual can fulfill the law of Christ. The term "carrying one another's burdens" empathy was first introduced in 1909 by psychologist Edward B. Titchener as a translation of the German term einfühlung (meaning "feeling into"). Several different theories have been proposed to explain empathy (Titchener)[19]. Cambridge Dictionary, defines "empathy as the ability to share someone else's feelings or experiences by imagining what it would be like to be in that person's situation." It went to say that "Lower levels of empathy may contribute to conflict in social interactions and thereby heighten levels of negative emotions experienced by some

---

[19] https://www.verywellmind.com/edward-b-titchener-biography-2795526

children."[20] Unfortunately, some surveys indicate "that empathy is on the decline in the western world, like United States, United Kigdom and Europe. The findings that motivate parents, schools, and communities to support programs that help people of all ages enhance and maintain their ability to "walk in each other's shoes." According to the [21]Merriam-Webster Dictionary, empathy is:"the action of understanding, being aware of, being sensitive to, and vicariously experiencing the feelings, thoughts, and experience of another of either the past or present without having the feelings, thoughts, and experience fully communicated in an objectively explicit manner; also: the capacity for this". In [22]"PositivePsychology" One recent neuroscience paper defines empathy as "a multifaceted construct used to account for the capacity to share and understand the thoughts and feelings of others" (Decety & Yoder, 2016).[23] The authors of this paper go on to highlight a few aspects of empathy, including what they call emotional empathy and cognitive empathy, an important distinction in academic work involving empathy. They describe emotional empathy as "the capacity to share or become affectively aroused by others' emotional states at least in valence and intensity", and they describe cognitive empathy as "the ability to consciously put oneself into the mind of another person to understand what he [or she] is thinking or feeling". To put it another way, according to that way of thinking, empathy can be broken into at least two parts: "feeling" the way someone else feels, and "understanding" how someone else feels. In nutshell individuals need not to ompose their values to other people and it may lead to dysfunctionality in the family system.

In other words, empathy is made up of being able to put yourself in someone else's position both intellectually and emotionally. This is just one (incomplete) way of breaking down empathy and there are several other interesting definitions. For our purposes, we can keep

---

[20] https://dictionary.cambridge.org/dictionary/english/empathy
[21] https://www.merriam-webster.com/dictionary/empathy
[22] https://positivepsychology.com/
[23] https://positivepsychology.com/empathy/

it simple and consider empathy to be the ability to put yourself in someone else's position to understand how they are feeling, as well as being sensitive to how someone else is feeling. One study found that psychotherapy clients "viewed empathy as integral to the personal and professional relationship they had with their psychotherapist", and believed that empathy from their psychotherapist benefited their psychotherapy sessions (Macfarlane et al., 2017)[24]. Some of the specific benefits of empathy listed by clients included greater levels of trust between the client and therapist, a greater level of self-understanding for the client, and higher levels of feeling happy and secure.

The ability to share the thoughts, feelings, recognize and understand another individual is very essential for behaving compassionately and very important for a healthy and functional relationship. To establish positive relationships, it is crucial to have this ability to convey support for a partner, relative, or friend. In relationship, this actually involves experiencing your partner's point of view, rather than just your own point of view, and enables good chosen pattern of behaviour that from within the heart and not imposed or compelled attitude. This does not indicate an individual should neglect his or her personal needs and become a victim of his or her partner. It also does not give a license for an individual to take advantage of his [or her] partner. It simply gives an individual the opportunity to receive support, feel being heard, esperince another person's lovely presence and emotional care.

Relationship can be further cemented by the empathic ability to assume the cognitive state of another individual, i.e "see the problem through the eyes of a partner." I strongly believe that in a healthy relationship, we should expect an individual to empathize with his [or her] partner during difficult moments, personal struggles, crisis, hard times and even during good times. Some experts suggests that showing empathy for an individual's positive emotion, is more beneficial for satisfaction in relationship

According to "SAGE JOURNAL" – "The Journal of Patient

---

[24] https://positivepsychology.com/empathy/

Experience" in the article "The Science of Empathy" by Helen Riess, MD, she quoted Maya Angelou saying, "I've learned that people will forget what you said, people will forget what you did, but people will never forget how you made them feel" (Riess).[25] In one study, displaying empathy for a partner's positive emotions was five times more beneficial for relationship satisfaction than only empathizing with his or her negative emotions. "Self- and other-empathy leads to replenishment and renewal of a vital human capacity. If we are to move in the direction of a more empathic society and a more compassionate world, it is clear that working to enhance our native capacities to empathize is critical to strengthening individual, community, national, and international bonds."According to [26]Empathy Lab, "Empathy day June is 9, 2020. It was founded in 2017, by not-for-profit Empathy Lab, who are on the mission to inspire the rising generation to drive a new empathy movement. Empathy is a vital human force which has come into sharp focus during the pandemic." Research indicates people can choose to cultivate and prioritize empathy. People who spend more time with individuals different from themselves tend to adopt a more empathic outlook outlook toward others. Other research finds that reading novels can help foster the ability to put ourselves in the minds of others. Meditation has also been shown to help cultivate brain states that increase empathy. "The practice of empathy begins with directing loving-kindness, or compassion, toward one's self. As a sense of respect, friendship, and love or compassion develops with oneself, the practice then expands to include others". An extract from the article [27]"The Science of Empathy" by Helen Riess, MD, "Studies have shown that specific areas of the brain play a role in how empathy is experienced. More recent approaches focus on the cognitive and neurological processes that lie behind empathy. Researchers have found that different regions of the brain play an important role in empathy, including the anterior cingulate cortex

[25] https://journals.sagepub.com/doi/full/10.1177/2374373517699267

[26] https://www.empathylab.uk/empathy-day.

[27] https://journals.sagepub.com/doi/full/10.1177/2374373517699267

and the anterior insula. Research suggests that there are important neurobiological components to the experience of empathy."

A relationship needs to be healthy, both emotional health and physical health. There is no doubt that an individual accepting to take his [or her] partner's perspective has so many benefits, but most especially in the case of disagreement, a little more effort to understand their perspective, is essential for long lasting love relationship. This is important because it is easier during crisis or hard times to focus on an individual's negative qualities instead of making a conscious effort to focus on his [or her] positive qualities. An attitude to see things from your partner's point of view would definitely eliminate discontent and make the relationship stronger and healthier. In a relationship in which everything always went along seamlessly there won't be any room for attraction and growth. When conflict is handled properly, and there is compromise, the relationship changes and growth is the result. Couples should be willing to create time and get to know each other by spending time in communication.

So supporting one another - Understanding your spouse weakness and assisting him [or her] demands the spirit of empathy. The ability to sense another person's emotions, coupled with the ability to imagine what someone else might be thinking or feeling. Relationship will become healthier when individuals learn in addition to just assigning the goof up accountability; going deeper to understand the other person's context goes a long way in providing feedback to peeson, coach him [or her] on right behaviours, improve communication, explore right fitment of the person to what he [she] like to do, and develop trust and respect. Delayed judgement is a behaviour where we hold back our instinct to judge someone based on visible cues like looks, dressing, speech and tone.

Every kind of trial - emotional burdens, financial difficulties, spiritual questions, physical pain, relational stresses - presents a new opportunity for a couple to persevere. According to Joel Osteen in the book "Break out!" – "Keep the right perspective," We all face challenges, but it's not the size of the problem that's important, it's our perception of that problem; it's how big or small we make it in our minds. If you see your challenges as impossible and you tell yourself and your spouse" (Osteen, 2014, 143).[28] We will never get out of debt and we will never accomplish our dreams, then your wrong perspective can keep you from becoming all God's created you to be. When you focus on, you magnify. If you stay focused on your problem or what you don't have and how it will never work out, all you're doing is making it bigger than it really is. When youy magnify something you don't change the size of the object; you only change the perception of it.

Commitment helps you stay connected to each other through trials; perseverance is the determination to outlast the problems, to help each other get to the other side. Think of the intimacy and friendship that can develop in your relationship when you are committed to persevering through every trial. Do not judge anyone from whats apparent. Facing trials requires a depth of trust that doesn't grow overnight. This is why the trust of adopting measures and approaches to ensure a healthy relationship requires love that grows richer over time, as couples prove themselves trustworthy to one another. It may be true that trust begins to build during courtship, and commitment to trust may be inherent in the wedding vows. But complete trust is established over time and under the pressure of daily life. Learn to understand other person better. Go below the surface of the iceberg that each one of us are. Your ability to understand your partner and connect with him [or her] will make your relationship to be filled with effectiveness, commitment, trust; and happiness. You will learn from your partner's life experiences and contexts; you will help him [or her] to grow, and you will enrich each other.

---

[28] Osteen, Joel. *Break Out!: and Live an Extraordinary Life* .FaithWords, 2014, P.143).

SIX

Recognizing and Celebrating of Achievement in the Relationship

A healthy relationship should have room for growth. Relationships become stagnant not just because a certain amount of time spent together, but because both parties, as couples or as individuals feel stuck, stagnant and without progress. Couples in a relationship will not remain exactly the same for a long time. Individuals have aspirations, interests, hopes, goals and visions which constantly evolved or are updated. This is not an excuse for an unhealthy relationship because both couples should accommodate the opportunity for growth. An individual who thwarts the professional or personal goals or vision of his [or her] partner, with doubt and de-motivational attitude is not wise. An individual that has a vision to own his [or her] own business, must not lose <u>confidence</u> to pursue them further because of the attitude of the partner. Talent, smart and hard-working individual should be encouraged and celebrated by their partners.

The achievement of a partner should not be seen as threat to the relationship. Couples who demonstrate they care about their partner at least as much as they care about themselves, i.e. their partner's happiness is their happiness. These are couples who love to take care of each other's needs as they arise without complain and for the sake of love demonstrates kindness, selflessness by recognizing and celebrating each other's achievement in the relationship. Relationships and people grow and change over time. Individual should share achievement and be glad that their partner is really doing well. The things that make a big difference, in life is sharing time spent together to celebrate each other's success, which is a way to regularly celebrating your relationship.

In the book "Become a Better you" by Joel Osteen the author encouraged individuals to be free with your compliments and be quick to vocalize them. I quote "Remember, your thoughts don't bless anybody but you. You can think good thoughts about somebody all day long, but it's not going to do them one bit of good. You must vocalize those thoughts; speak them out. Everyday, try to find somebody you can compliment, someone that you can build up. If a waiter at the restaurant gives you good service, don't just think about it. Tell him. "thanks for being such a fine waiter and taking good care of us today," Those positive words might make his day. Our society overflows with critics, cynics, and faultfinders. Many people quickly point what you are doing wrong, but relatively few take the time to point out anything you are doing right (Osteen, 2010, 143–145).[29] I want to build up people and not tear them down. I'm going to do my best to leave places better off than they were before I passed by. Friend choose to bring out the best in the people that God has put in your life. You're never more like God than when you give, and the closer thing to His heart is helping others (love or celebrate others). If you will be a people builder, focused on bringing out the best in others, I can promise you this: God will bring out the best in you."

Recognizing and celebrating of achievement in the relationship is showing your partner that you are proud of his [or her] achievements, no matter how small, big, great, important they may be, is a really powerful way to strengthen the relationship. This way you show them that what is important for them, is also important to you. Love is sharing the goals or dreams of your partner and encouraging them along the way of accomplishing that plan is also really important to make the relationship strong and healthy. This is love in action.

---

[29] Osteen, Joel. *Become a Better You: 7 Keys to Improving Your Life Every Day.* Running Press Book Publishers, 2010.

Celebrating your partner will also help both couples to keep your focus on the positive sides in the relationship rather than the negatives, flaws, and failures. In my research, I discovered that couples who prefer pointing out the negatives, faults and failures in their relationship instead of showing their celebrating their achievement do not stay together for long, because every individual love to be appreciated and celebrated. This kind of behavior is very important for the relationship to become really healthy, because everyone has some form of imperfection, and an individual who learns to fully accept the imperfections of his [or her] partner and celebrate the achievements, no matter how small, big or great they are will surely enjoy a healty and successful relationship. I think that is what love is all about, is it? Ofcourse it is.

My suggestion is that couples should take time celebrating their achievement as partners in the relationship, and this can be done by simply taking the time to regularly reminisce together about what both partners have accomplished or achieved together, as a couple. They can encourage themselves with their successes and achievement together in this journey of life. This will put more spark or life into your relationship, couples taking the decision to regularly share, enjoy and celebrate with their partner what both have done together as a couple. A lovely way to remember that couples are not only partners but in love and in it together for good and we will continue to strengthen and encourage the bond with each other. The scripture says in Proverbs 27:17, "As iron sharpens iron, so one person sharpens another." Many years ago, one iron blade was used to sharpen another blade until both became more effective tools. This visual aid of a common implement of work or war provides a practical model for many human relationships.

The process of helping an individual improve his [or her] effectiveness absolutely requires a positive relationship. Faithful are the wounds of a friend, but deceitful are the kisses of an enemy. We know this concept to be true. It is much better to accept Godly advice or even constructive criticism from someone we know, a partner, someone we love, and someone we know that cares about us, than it is from a stranger or simple acquaintance. We want to know that the person giving us the counsel has our best interest at heart. That's why it is so important for each of us to build growing relationships with others in life. We all need someone who can help us rub off the hard edges, honestly have our best interests in mind when they do it and celebrate our successes or archievements. There are times when these sharpening conversations, even from loving partner, can come across as harsh, mean, or judgmental. But it definitely helps to know that these people care and that they have a genuine interest in helping us improve and be successful in life.

What is really vital for a healthy relationship is that the partners express their true feelings rather than hiding them. It is normal that couples don't agree on every single thing but appreciating the way of thinking of their partner and trying to understand their point of view is a must for every healthy relationship. Many couples forget how important that actually is, so they criticize instead of encouraging their partners and hurting their feelings leads to closing up and not willing to share their opinions, emotions, goals, and visions. Recognizing and celebrating of achievement in the relationship, is in my own opinion one of the small things in life which actually is not that small at all, it is like the small salt but very valuable, certainly if it is used properly, because it brings a lot of joy and gladness to a relationship. Giving encouragement to your partner most especially when they are feeling discouraged, fall short or even fail will be definitely appreciated. In that way you show your love and care for them and that you would do anything to make them successful and happy. Recognizing and celebrating of achievement in the Relationship is healthy while blaming, fault finding or shaming is very unhealthy or destructive. The opposite of blame is praise, where somebody is praised for doing something well or within values. In particular praise is due when a person has helped others while disadvantaging themselves. This contrasts with blame when they help themselves but harm others. This will be addressed in the next chapter.

SEVEN

Non-judgmental or non-shaming approach

Blaming is to hold responsible, find fault with, to lace the responsibility for a fault, error, etc. Blame is an accusation that a person has committed a misdeed. The misdeed is usually an undesirable act that goes against the value of the accuser. It is often a specific act, such as doing or saying something. In blaming, the accuser is positioning themselves as morally superior. Shaming is making someone worthless in the eye of the accuser. Shaming takes it further than blaming by publicly humiliate or sham someone for being or doing something specified. Blaming and shaming are in the family as well as church family. Both Blaming and shaming never resolved anything, rather they create emotional hurts. Blaming is something that started from the time of Adam. In the scripture Genesis 3:11-13" And he said, who told thee that thou wast naked? Hast thou eaten of the tree, whereof I commanded thee that thou shouldest not eat? And the man said, the woman whom thou gravest to be with me, she gave me of the tree, and I did eat. And the Lord God said unto the woman, what is this that thou hast done? And the woman said, the serpent beguiled me, and I did eat. So, the scriptures reveals that Adam ate the forbidden fruit, he pointed finger to Eva when he was confronted by God, Thus, "the woman you gave to be with me, she gave me of the tree and I did eat."

Non-judgmental or non-shaming approach in a relationship

could be called "respect." This concept is not only associate with individuals that are not intimate with each other like elders, law and order, religious ministers, indvidual's faith and authority, but most importantly within a close partnership or couple. In healthy relationships, couples should not belittle debase or invalidate one another. Each partner most value his [or her] partner's time and opinions like he [or she] value their own. Couples must realize that to love also means to protect each other's privacy and boundaries.

In this book "Healing the Dysfunctional Church family," the author dealt with issues that create more problems without the necessary resolution to the issue. Some are emotional charged statements that results from listening to inflammatory statement about neighbours, church members and ministers. Blaming could be very destructive and demoralizing (Main, 1992, 34-35).[30] Jesus Christ should always be our example in every aspect of life. Let us look at two important stories in the scripture. Stories that reveals that Jesus is a loving and accepting God, and we should follow His example. The story of the woman, called the "Samaritan woman at the well" The story is found according to the scripture in John 4:4-42. Jesus had to go through Samaria city called Sychar, near the plot of ground that Jacob had given his son Joseph. Jesus in this case encounter broke three Jewish customs, spoke to woman alone and a fornicator, a Samaritan, ask her for a drink of water, although using the same jar or cup to the Jews is ceremonially unclean. He told the woman He could give her living water and revealed Himself as the messiah to her despite her sin. That gentleness and kindness changed the woman's life for ever, that she was transformed and went and invited the people to come and see a man who told her all that she ever did. She was not ashamed or condemned but changed for the best due to the love of God. The other story is found in the scripture in John 7:53-8:11, Jesus and the woman taken in adultery is a beautiful illustration of Jesus silencing his critics while graciously addressing a

---

[30] Mains, David. Healing the Dysfunctional Church Family. Victor Books – SP Publications. Inc, 19925, (p34-35)

sinner filled with guilt and shame and in need of grace and mercy."
He wrote something on the ground and the woman's accusers were
unable to handle it and they left the woman alone. Jesus never blamed
the woman caught for committing adultery, but he offered a way for
her to escape the shameful and humiliating situation by saying, In
these two stories Jesus saved the two women destinies in ways that
are gentle and constructive without blaming or shaming. Blaming
is evil, but shaming is even worse and destructive. These skills
are commonly passed in dysfunctional families. These blaming and
shaming traits, that is dysfunctional in nature can be also manifest
in the church, which leads to finger pointing, fault shifting, within
the church families. This fault shifting or blaming other people is
simply done to redirect focus to others instead of accepting blame.
It is wrong to focus on the problems of others while we ignore our
own problems or simply fail to accept or addressed them properly.

A relationship without respect is damaged and it takes a long and
painful effort to build it back properly. However, it very important
for a healthy relationship that the partners express their true feelings
rather than hiding them. It is normal if they don't agree on every
single thing, but appreciating the way of thinking of the partner and
trying to understand their point of view is not an option but a must
for good relationship. Respecting your partner or non-judgmental or
non-shaming approach, can be viewed in different ways: respecting
your partner's time, heart, character, and trust.

In an article titled "How to Be Non-Judgmental in a Judgmental
World," written by Emily Chee Wah, a professional coach and founder
of "YourLifePathCo," in the section "instructed learning to express
your need and values, rather than labelling something, someone, or a
situation as bad or good or right."[31] She says in reference to Dr. Marshall
Rosenberg's in his book, "Nonviolent Communication: A Language
of Life," calls this "Moralistic Judgments". He writes that "blame,
insults, put-downs, labels, criticism, comparisons, and diagnoses are
all forms of judgment." He postures that when you disagree with

---

[31] https://yourlifepathco.com/

something or someone and you use any of these forms to express your disagreement, you are being judgmental. Expressing judgment like this, puts you and the other party diametrically opposite one another, which creates conflict, aggression or defensiveness (Rosenberg, 2015).[32] One side must win at the expense of the other. Instead, by learning to express differences without blaming etc. or making the other party bad or wrong, you can discover a key to having dialogue and a bridge towards mutual respect and acceptance. The way you might do that according to Dr. Rosenberg is by connecting to "what you are feeling, fearing, yearning for, or missing" that is present to you in the moment because of the situation. Rather than go to blame, comparison etc. choose to communicate the feeling instead as a way to open and invite dialogue.

However, there are many things people do in relationships that can break down respect, like name-calling, talking negatively about the other to friends or family, and threatening to leave the relationship. Judging people is a bad habit or behavior that is toxic to a relationship, because individuals are different and does act differently depending on the situation, circumstances and people. So judging people should be discouraged in a relationship. When communicating an individual will usually reveal as much of themselves as they would like to based on the circumstances, so you cannot identify the personality of an individual simply based on feeling because nobody knows deeply down, on the inside what is going on with their lives at that moment. An individual that wants his [or her] partner to think more like him [or her] does, makes the partner feel not knowledgeable and consistently try to make partner change his [or her] mind about something important by controlling spirit is not interested in a healthy relationship. This behavior is dysfunctional because it is very controlling and does not promote healthy relationship.

In the book by Billy Graham "The Inspiration Writings" – "Peace with God"; "The Secret of Happiness"; "Answers to Life's Problems",

---

[32] Rosenberg, Marshall B. *Nonviolent Communication: a Language of Life.* Puddledancer Press, 2015.

The Bible says that our obligation to each other as Christians is such that we should be example to each other. Apostle Paul said, "Be thou an example of the believers, in conversation, in charity, in spirit, in faith, in purity." This is not a suggestion – it is a command! It is not recommendation, but an obligation (Graham, 2017, 261).[33] We are to be model Christians. The bible also says we are to forgive one another. "And be ye kind one to another tenderhearted forgiving one another, even as God for Christ's sake hath forgiven you." Jesus said that if you will not forgive, neither will your father which is in heaven forgive your sins. He also said, "When ye stand praying, forgive, if you have ought against any; that your Father also may forgive you," We are told as Christians not to judge one another, but rather decide never to put a sumbling block or hindrance in the way of a brother.

A couple that is in a non-judgmental or non-shaming approach relationship, are free to discuss difficult issues without fighting even when they disagree. It is not wrong for couples to have occasional fights, but tbey must be able discuss important issues without a partner going into a rage of uncontrolled anger. Putting yourself first is essential for growing into a successful and content individual but not being self-centered and blind for the presence of a partner's problems and opinion. A partner who has controlling spirit, skilled manipulators at making the other partner own emotions work in his [or her] favour, may not be judgmental but is shaming, manipulating the partner into feeling a steady stream of guilt about any difficult problem or issue is not healthy. The partner with the controlling spirit manova issues to his [or her] advantage because the other partner, will gradually do whatever it takes to avoid feeling guilty. This could means relenting and giving up power and their own dissenting opinion within the relationship, which plays right into the hand of the controlling partner.

The solution should be anytime, an individual finds himself

---

[33] Graham, Billy. *The Inspiration Writings: Peace With God - The Secret of Happiness - Answers to Life's Problems*. Inspirational Press New York, 2017, (P261).

wanting to blame his [or her] partner or something else for his [or her] thoughts, feelings or actions, shout take a moment to exercise the power of choice on how you respond. Keeping in mind that everyone and nobody else is responsible for him [or her] thoughts, feelings and actions (despite what he [or she] might say to the partner). Choosing to take personal responsibility instead of putting the blame on the partner or an external party, will result in others viewing him [or her] as a person of integrity and will be more open to what it is him [or her] have to say.

EIGHT

Sharing of values or Responsibilities

Couples in a healthy, loving relationship are expected to demonstrate to one another trust, truth, love, taken responsibility of our words, action and when necessary the will to change. Therefore, in the context of a relationship it is of fundamental importance that an individual take responsibility for his [or her] own happiness, must be realistic knowing that every relationship has disagreements and days when staying isn't the easiest choice, learn to admit their mistakes and faults, acknowledge they have done something to hurt their partner, (intentionally or not), and above all make good their words because healthy, stable relationships have a sense of reciprocity built into them.

In the book "He came first" by Rod Parsely, I quote: some Christians are guided by motto "if it jams, force it. If it breaks, it needed fixing anyway" (Parsely, 2002, 141).[34] They try to make things happen because they're too impatient to wait on God. They confront people's sin without waiting on God's direction. And in the process they hurt themselves and often the people around them. If what you're doing isn't working, then stop doing it. Stop preaching the way you've been preaching. Stop depending on what youìve been depending on. Stop praying the way you've been praying if the answer was in that, you wouldn't be in bondage right now.

---

[34] Parsley, Rod. *He Came First: Following Christ to Spiritual Breakthrough*. T. Nelson Publishers, 2002, (P141).

You would be in freedom. Obviously, the way you're doing it isn't working, so maybe it's time to wait on God and do it His way.

It is most important that couples take time not only to look out for each other but to look out for the best of each other, and should put a complete stop to bean-count every little time a partner does something to help the other out. If one partner always keeps tag or score card of every last interaction within your relationship for what ever reason that could be, for example demand a favor in return or holding a grudge., this is not the Sharing of values we meant but could very well be his [or her] way of having the upper hand, in which case it could become downright exhausting.

Boundaries help us to determine who is responsible for what. If we understand who owns what we then know who must take responsible for it. If we can discover who is responsiblde for what we have an opportunity for change. When we see that the problem is ours, and we are responsible for it, then we are able to seek for change, because responsibility involves action. For any thing to happen, we need to take action. We need to change some attitude, behaviour, reaction, or choices. Each partner must actively participate in the resolution of whatever relational problem we might have, even if it is not our fault because anger and a lack of boundaries are linked together. Responsibility shows us that we are the ones who must work through our feelings and learn how to feel differently because our attitudes and not those of our partner causes us to feel distressed and powerless. Boundaries help us to determine who is responsible for what. If we understand who owns what we then know who must take responsible for it. If we can discover who is responsible for what we have an opportunity for change. When we see that the problem is ours, and we are responsible for it, then we are able to seek for change, because responsibility involves action (Cloud & Townsend, 1999, 123-130).[35]

In healthy relationship, reciprocity is based on trust and partners

---

[35] Cloud, Henry, and John Sims Townsend. *Boundaries in Marriage*. Zondervan, 1999 (P123-130).

love sharing of values. Trusting equilibrium takes its place in healthy atmosphere were both couples just generally love to serve or do for each other when needed. In a healthy relationships, neither partner should feels resentful and as long as both partners feel comfortable with the level sharing of values or simply said the "give-and-take" which they practice. This said and done but the importance of of ownership in a healthy and loving relationship cannot be over emphasied. When we identify the boundaries in a relationship i.e. we identify who "owns" things such as attitudes, behaviours and feelings, then we can identify to whom they "belong". In the case of an issue or problem in one of these areas, to identify whom the problem belong is possible.

A relationship like marriage requires each partner to have a sense of ownership of himself [or herself]. Any attempt to control the life of a partner is harmful to the relastionship. We cannot blam others for our own behaviour, we must take responsibility or ownership for own actions and behaviour. When neither partner took personal ownership of his [or her] behaviour, and believed in their minds, that their behaviour was literally "caused" by the other person. In one of the case studies, Joe claimed that "his anger was due to his partner's behaviour, rather than accept his too immaturity to respond to her more helpfully and a deep need some help. There must be need for an individual to love his [or her] partner correctly no matter his or her behaviour.

Responsibility demands that the individual receiving counsel or advice must be willing to allow his [or her] partner to look for the vulnerabilities in his [or her] life, accept what they point out, and then do something to fix the problem or issue revealed. This principle of responsibility leads to helpful and real conversations which grow out of growing, loving, and constructive relationships. In a close relationships were trust and respect exist, couples should accept when their partner identify some weak areas in their lives and willing to address those areas together. This does not give couples permission to have critical and negative attitude, that delights in pointing out the faults of their partner.

Couples should desire what is best for each other; but to build on that concept, they should sincerely wants to share with each other's growth and also sincerely desire what is best for one another, then it is imperative for each partner to accept the constructive criticism with an attitude of willingness and acceptance and take the responsibility to do everything possible to improve. Sharing of values could lead to the pointing out each others weakness, even trends that could be difficult in the lives of the couple, but it bring strong bonding, greater level of understanding and knowing and taking responsibility for the right things that should be done to solve the situation or issue.

That's why situations like this should motivate couples back to the life-changing word of life or the truth of God's word. God can use the "wounds of a partner" to motivate an individual, to sharpen his [or her], and to provide or promote some responsibility for their lives. However, true victory and lasting progress comes only from God Himself. The scripturs say, in Hebrew 4:12, "For the word of God is alive and active. Sharper than any double-edged sword, it penetrates even to dividing soul and spirit, joints and marrow; it judges the thoughts and attitudes of the heart." While the word of life goes further to illustrate in the scriptures says in 2 Timothy 3:16-17, "All Scripture is inspired by God and profitable for teaching, for reproof, for correction, for training in righteousness; so that the man of God may be adequate, equipped for every good work." God will use the convicting power of His Holy Spirit and the word of God to rebuke an individual of the sinful and harmful practices in his [or her] lives.

The wonderful and good thing about it, is that God never just points out weaknesses without providing a solution. God's word will help an individual "correct" the problem and will provide the step-by-step "instructions" needed to go on living "in righteousness." We must highly value and build Godly and growing relationships with a partner who shares our values and faith in Jesus Christ, who can exhort us to a closer walk with Him, but our relationships and the resulting conversations and discussions must drive us back to the Word of God or better still the Word of Life, where our loving and gracious Heavenly Father gives us true life-changing strategies.

NINE

Restoration/Redemption

Restoration is renewal, revival, or re-establishment to a former, original, normal, or unimpaired condition; restitution of something taken away or lost. Redemption is the act of atoning for a fault, sin, mistake or guilt; being delivered, rescued. God, therefore, seeks to demonstrate in every generation to every individual His sovereignty and redemption in the midst of conflict, adversity and social iniquity. In addition, His aim is to establish a personal relationship with us to experience His love and power, justice and righteousness, grace and truth to sustain us in hope as we navigate through the trials of life. God hopes for us to experience a measure of His redemption and glory "on earth as it is in heaven." Ezra understood this reality. He prayed to God to open our eyes to "give us a measure of revival in our bondage." Paul understood it even more, having been enlightened and filled by the Holy Spirit. He realized that the Holy Spirit, God's presence and power within us, seals us with gifts and measures of God's grace as down payments of our future eternal inheritance. The scripture says, in Ephesians 1:13-14 "And when you heard the word of truth (the gospel of your salvation) when you believed in Christ you were marked with the seal of the promised Holy Spirit, who is the down payment of our inheritance, until the redemption of God's own possession, to the praise of his glory." So how does God bring restoration and redemption to us on earth as it is in heaven? Restoration in God's eyes relates to being restored to His original intentions; what He intended for us. His goal is to refresh us, relieve us of pressure and tension, help us recover things lost and reverse a bad course you may find yourself on.

God will challenge our conscience and will. However, He always points to redemption and restoration. Therefore, God delights in us asking, seeking and knocking; in hope of us finding our way and joy in His love in Him. So it challenges us to be seekers of truth in all things. Knowing God's love, therefore, enables us to be honest about our own sinfulness and shortcomings. It enables us to come clean before God and be living testimonies of God's grace. In the book "Healing of Memories (Prayer and Confession Steps to Inner healing) by Matthew Linns, S.J. & Dennis Linns, the author helps us to understand more clearly the power of Redemption and Restoration to the mankind. The power to heal is evident symbolically in the refreshing coolness that accompanies forgiveness. The author refers to his experience as therapist in a psychiatric clinic. And having directed retreats and workshops, would be amazed if this rite of forgiveness did not heal everyone either physically, mentally or spiritually. Forgiveness bring healing. When individual forgave those, who hurt or offend them, parents, neighbours, even themselves and God, it brings healing (Linns, 1974, 8).[36] The healing power of forgiveness is from the finished work of Jesus. The Word of God teaches us that in bringing many sons unto glory (God's power, goodness, and present), Jesus was made the captain of our salvation perfect through sufferings. The scripture says, Hebrew 2:9-11 "But we do see Him who was made for a little while lower than the angels, namely, Jesus, because of the suffering of death crowned with glory and honor, so that by the grace of God He might taste death for everyone. For it was fitting for Him, for whom are all things, and through whom are all things, in bringing many sons to glory, to perfect the author of their salvation through sufferings. For both He who sanctifies and

---

[36] Linns, S.J, and Lines, D. Healing of Memories: Prayer and Confession Steps to Inner healing. Paulist Press – New York / Mahwah, N.J., 1974, (P8).

those who are sanctified are all from one Father; for which reason He is not ashamed to call them brethren."

Flexibility in relationships take compromise and the key point is that both partners show flexibility in day-to-day life and decision-making, because if it is just one partner always doing the bending, that imbalance can grow toxic over time. In healthy relationships, both partners are willing to adjust as needed to the changes and growth i.e. positive and negative during a long-term relationship. Both couples must be able to evaluate on a joint level, especially during conflicts, what matters most to each person within the relationship, and how that should be prioritized. Two partners who are never willing to bend to meet the other will be on separate paths altogether before long, which is a far cry from truly sharing a life together.

Restoration and redemption are possible where both couples are willing to work together, showing flexibility to adjust for the love of one another. Restoration and redemption should not be used as weapons of control or power struggle in a healthy relationship. Controlling people may come on very strongly in the beginning with seemingly romantic gestures. But upon closer inspection, many of those gestures, extravagant gifts, expectations of serious commitment early on, taking the partner out for luxurious meals or on adventurous outings, letting the partner have full use of their car or home when they're not there and paying off the partner's debts, can be used to control. Specifically, they create an expectation of the other partner giving something in return, or a sense that he [or she] feels beholden to that individual because of all the favour. This is not redemption in love.

No individual should use redemption to make he [or she] partner feel that they have done something wrong even before they realize what went wrong. There is advance judgement and decision of wrongdoing to a point that an individual may feel they've got a whole case against his [or her] partner who needs restoration. It cannot be used as justification for punishing an individual or preemptively trying to keep a partner from making that "error" again or wrongly to keep a partner acting in ways suitable to just one party. So redemption and restoration demands couples who are really listening to each other's cares, concerns about what their partner have to say and what matters to him [or her].

Couples have to invest time, attention, interest and their memory power to seek restoration and redemption for their relationship to be successful, healthy and better in particular and for a long joyful and happy time of relationship in general. Couple that listens to each other are genuinely connect, hear the unspoken as well as what is verbalized and are simply a lot happier. If your partner does not think it is important for dialogue and conversations, it's an excellent sign that such individual in a relationship without communication is not a solid partner. In a healthy relationship, were both couples feel good about being together, there must be communication which enables restoration and redemption. It's the kind of love described by the apostle Paul: "Love never gives up, never loses faith, is always hopeful, and endures through every circumstance"

TEN

Repentance/Remorse and Apreciation

Repentance involves a change in the way we think and act. It results in a change in lifestyle. The normal New Testament use of this word involves a change from a sinful way of life to a way of life that honours God. Remorse may accompany the admission of wrongdoing, but it can also be present when nothing wrong has been done. It focuses on the consequences or effects of one's actions on others, but does not necessarily imply that those consequences were caused by wrongdoing.[37] The scriptures says in 2 Corinthians 7:8-9, "For though I caused you sorrow by my letter, I do not regret it; though I did regret it - for I see that that letter caused you sorrow, though only for a while - now rejoice, not that you were made sorrowful, but that you were made sorrowful to the point of repentance; for you were made sorrowful according to the will of God, so that you might not suffer loss in anything through us." In this context remorse is contrasted with gladness or joy.

An individual could be hurt or angry at God, his [or her] partner, even himself [or herself] for the death of a baby or someone they love, on the other hand it may lead to a partner new appreciation life and a desire to share it with neighbours. The pain from a broken friendship or marriage could keep an individual from ever opening deeply again to another person. The Holy Spirit of God help us in our weakness, with memories that open us up to recall in our heart the feeling of

---

[37] https://www.journal33.org/index.html

love, peace and joy. According to the author of the research book "Healing of Memories: Prayer and Confession Steps to Inner healing by Lines, we could every moment in two ways; one, it could open us to God, our neighbour and yourself. Or two, it could close us to the point of needing psychiatric help. In healing of Memories, we take those memories that cripple us and look at them also from the Spirit's viewpoint (Linns, 1974, 60).[38]

So change in one's actions can be associated with remorse, though this does not always occur. When it does, the biggest difference between the words "remorse" and "repentance" might be the emphasis. (The one would emphasize the sadness, while the other would emphasize the changes in conduct). Repentance is the more permanent of the two. Remorse can be temporary. The absence of remorse can be quite permanent. For those who may be interested in the original New Testament Greek: The word group related to "metanoeo" is normally translated as repentance, or repent. The word group related to "metamelomai" is normally translated as remorse.

The research about the importance of gratitude within relationship published by the [39]"Greater Good Science Center at UC Berkeley" is striking, it makes us feel the effect of "chronic criticism" even for small things. Criticism, like isolation, is something that starts gradually, that an individual may take the criticism as not warranted, or may understand that their partner is just trying to help them be a better person. On the other hand, they may try to rationalize it, and decided it is not a problem and nothing to be taken personally. But ultimately, no matter how individually small a criticism seems, if it's part of a constant dynamic within a relationship, it would be very tough to feel accepted, loved, or validated. If every little thing an individual does could use improvement in his [or her] partner's eyes, then how is the individual valued as a true equal, let alone loved unconditionally. Teasing, humour and even lack of apreciation can be a fundamental mode of interacting within many long-term

---

[38] Linns, S.J, and Lines, D. Healing of Memories: Prayer and Confession Steps to Inner healing. Paulist Press – New York / Mahwah, N.J, 1974, (p60).

[39] http://ihd.berkeley.edu/research-centers/greater-good-science-center

relationships. The key aspect is whether it feels comfortable and loving to both parties.

Where there is pain or hurt due to lack of repentance, remorse and appreciation. We look unto the author and finisher of our faith. When we ask Christ to help us become thankful for a memory, we are requesting Him to take our focus off the painful memory and help us appreciate ourselves, more considerate of how we can serve our people like Joseph, when it gives us new vision to find God's way as did the disciples at Emmaus, then we have co-operated with Christ in uprooting the controlling hurt and planting His love. When we appreciate God's gifts in our lives, then we begin to see circumstances and situation about our lives His ways (Linns, 1974, 38).[40] The scripture says in Ephesian 2:10 "For we are his workmanship, created in Christ Jesus unto good works, which God hath before ordained that we should walk in them. {ordained: or, prepared}"

Couples that desire healthy and happy relationships, should not be thinly veiled and should take personally, the lack of repentance, remorse and appreciation. True repentance, genuine remorse and appreciation gives an individual true happiness and makes him [or her] more secure with his [or her] partners. The more an individual feels that gratitude, the more he [or she] feels appreciated for within relationships, which also improves the overall relationship's well-being. An expressions of repentance, gratitude and appreciation can help improve relationship satisfaction. A little word like "thank you" for something a partner does, indicates our gratitude and love and a lack of appreciation over time, produces a negative feeling within a relationship. Couples should learn to share gratitude by taking moment together to talk about what each one <u>appreciate</u> about the other, simply by saying kind words, for example, "I appreciate you for."

According to Dr. Mark Richards, Prepare/Enrich Facilitator and Trainer [41]"Research shows that people who hear frequent appreciations

[40] Linns, S.J, and Lines, D. Healing of Memories: Prayer and Confession Steps to Inner healing. Paulist Press – New York / Mahwah, N.J, 1974, (P38).
[41] https://blog.prepare-enrich.com/2018/02/5-ways-to-celebrate-your-relationship/

feel better about themselves, produce more, and serve more. Feeling appreciated is important to healthy relationships and for couples. It's also important to one's sense of being valued. Whenever you share an appreciation with another, their brain hears the appreciation and releases dopamine. Dopamine is a neurochemical that, when released, produces a feeling of pleasure. How many "dopamine shots" do you give your spouses, and children each day? May we begin to value not just being appreciated, but appreciating."

Sometimes when we forget to let other persons in our lives know that we appreciate them, although we think about it, but we don't vocalize or show it. A couple I counselled, earlier this year, the husband told me that his wife knows that he loves her because they have been together married for 25 years, but she says she will at least love to hear him say "he loves her" a least just once in a year, instead of total silence. This is not uncommon in todays's romantic relationships, individuals who take for granted repentance and most especially appreciation, "kind words of gratitude." Couples should show their partners, that you love him [or her] with kind words of appreciation. This could be done with words, cards, flowers, acts of kindness, or more. Remember, a flower can keep the fights at bay, because that feelings of gratitude are tied to the motivation to maintain one's relationship.

ELEVEN

Sex in Marriage

S ex was designed for marriage, a unique experience to bind
husband and wife together in what the Bible calls a "<u>one flesh</u>"
unity. [42]The sexual relationship of a married couple, united in Jesus
Christ, reflects something both marvelous and sacred; the unity of
the soul with God. Sexual enjoyment in marriage is a gift of God to
be enjoyed all through life. It's not love itself, but God invented it as
a way to express love. The scripture says in Matthew 19:6 "So they
are no longer two, but one flesh. Therefore what God has joined
together, let no one separate." Any sex outside those boundaries is
sin. Marital sex is to be the consummation of a lifetime commitment
made by two people. In ancient times and in several different cultures,
wedding celebrations often included a "bedding ceremony," in which
the bride and groom retreated to the bedchamber to consummate
their marriage. They would return to the party afterwards, and the
celebration with friends and family would go on. The marriage was
not considered complete until the bride and groom experienced
sexual intimacy. Some years ago in the southern part of Italy white
bedseet with blood stains, washed and put out on the line to dry was
a sign of virginity. While that may seem a bit unthinkable according
today's modern standards, it does illustrate the value that many

---

[42] Palau, Luis, and Steve Halliday. *High Definition Life: Trading Life's Good for Gods
Best*. Revell, 2005.
https://www.amazon.com/High-Definition-Life-Trading-Lifes/dp/0800718658

cultures traditionally placed on virginity and marital sex. Because the sexual drive is so powerful, the Bible encourages marriage in order to avoid <u>sexual immorality</u>. The scripture says in 1 Corinthians 7:1-2 "Now concerning the things about which you wrote, it is good for a man not to touch a woman. But because of immoralities, each man is to have his own wife, and each woman is to have her own husband."

Marital sex is to be mutual and frequent so that husband and wife are not tempted to commit adultery. The scripture says in 1 Corinthians 7:5 "Do not deprive each other except perhaps by mutual consent and for a time, so that you may devote yourselves to prayer. Then come together again so that Satan will not tempt you because of your lack of self-control." The Bible gives detailed instructions about marriage, sexuality, and <u>divorce</u>. The bodies of a husband and wife belong to each other. "The husband should fulfill his marital duty to his wife, and likewise the wife to her husband. The wife does not have authority over her own body, but the husband. Likewise, the husband does not have authority over his own body, but the wife." This giving over of the body to the one we are committed to should eliminate any possibility of extramarital liaisons. When we understand that our bodies are not our own, that they've been pledged to a spouse, we can shut the door on any thoughts of loaning them to someone else.

<u>Marriage</u> was designed by God as a picture of the covenant relationship He wants with us. The scripture says in 2 Corinthians 11:2 " I am jealous for you with a godly jealousy. I promised you to one husband, to Christ, so that I might present you as a pure virgin to him. God places great importance on human sexuality because marital sex is the most intimate relationship two human beings can have. It is also a picture of the intimacy God created us to enjoy with Him. In marital sex, there is a giving over of the body, and in our spiritual relationship with God, we are to present our bodies as a living sacrifice. The sexual act is a consummation of the covenant made between and man and a woman. Covenants were always consummated with the shedding of blood and usually, blood is shed when virginity is lost. Marital sex is more than a means of procreation

and a safe outlet for our sexual drives. It is holy to God because it symbolizes the pure soul intimacy He wants to share with us.

Marital sex is the only sexual expression approved by our Creator. It should be treated as a sacred gift and enjoyed by husband and wife. We should guard our hearts and eyes from any outside temptations that try to sully or steal sexual intimacy. Pornography, extramarital affairs, divorce, and promiscuity all rob us of the beauty and value God wove into the sexual act. The scripture says, in Proverbs 5:15–19 "Drink waters from your own cistern. And fresh water from your own well" We cannot experience all God designed sexuality to be unless we save all sexual activities for marriage. Sex can be a barometer for your relationship's health and if sex in Christian marriage isn't running smoothly, there are typically some other problems as well. Let love, honour and gentleness rule for lots of Christian marriage intimacy ideas.

Couples come for counselling to overcome constant tiredness, overpacked schedules, hurts and hang-ups, and even hormonal imbalances so they can finally experience the closeness and intimacy in marriage. Consistency cultivates intimacy in sex, in marriage. Couples should not think about an exact frequency, but try to be generally consistent, because every type of marriage have the same need for consistency. There can be a lot of reasons why a couple is not in the mood to have sex. This could be pregnancy, babies, health and schedules, to name but a few. The principal thing is priority because sex in Christian marriage is important. In most marriages (much the case for every couple) one person in the relationship has a stronger desire for sex than the other, so I suggest it is right from time to time to meet one partner's physical needs without having a deep emotional connection. Most of the time it's the man who has the stronger physical need. So the wife of a man with a stronger sex drive and sometimes you just aren't there, permit yourselves to do something quick. While you don't want to make this the only way you have sex, it is a way to help him feel loved even on those days when you're completely exhausted and there's no other way it's going to work.

Gary Chapman in the book "The Five Love Languages: How to Express Heartfelt Commitment to Your Mate (Relationships)." He came up with the notion that men and women have five love languages. People have unique ways of feeling loved. There are words of affirmation, receiving gifts, quality time, acts of service, and physical touch. It's important to know which love language speaks to an individual, along with his [or her] partner. Telling each other what makes you feel loved and special helps both of couples stay connected. One of the reasons it creates intimacy is because they have literally nothing to hide from the other person. It's all out there. But that doesn't mean they both have to take things too seriously. When something awkward happens, they simply laugh about it together (Chaman, 1992).[43]

Furthermore, an individual should make sure he [or she] is attending to his [or her] partner's love language consistently. Couples who spend endless and wonderful time with one another love humour, smile and a good laugh, a similar sense of humour or not, both should love to laugh at jokes. They love to be together and have a lot in common and can really enjoy each other's company, brings sparks to their sex lives. However, sex in marriage can be disrupted by overactive jealousy, accusations, or paranoia. A partner can arguably be viewed as endearing, or a sign of how much they care or how attached they are, but when it becomes more intense, it can be scary and possessive. A partner who views every interaction you have as being flirtatious, is suspicious or threatened by multiple people you come in contact with, or faults you for innocent interactions because they may be "leading someone on" may be insecure, anxious, competitive or even paranoid. This perspective becomes ingrained within your relationship, and will definitely have a negative impact on sex in marriage.

Couples should find or create time for intimacy, although busy schedule can make intimate time becoming tricky and tidious,

---

[43] Chapman, Gary. he Five Love Languages: How to Express Heartfelt Commitment to Your Mate (Relationships). Warner faith, 1992.

especially for couples with young children, but this makes it more of a challenge to overcome. Although tired and exhausted at the night, couples must learn it is best to give one another a time frame, so that they can become more intimate it needs to begin before a certain time and open communication is important in a home with kids and a husband that works. It takes intentional actions to maintain deep affection by hand holding, hugging, caressing, being close and simply sitting together holding hands can often be just as special.

Sex in marriage is also couple taking the responsibility and time to create a nice atmosphere for each other at home after being out working all day is a lovely way to have a date at home. There is no need to go anywhere, let the house be in an atmosphere of love with candles burning, a nice meal, unity, happiness, care and purposeful in serving one another with love. When a partner had a rough day, be intentional to do something that will encourage him [or her] to feel good or better. Maybe it is a cup of tea, chocolate drinks, a cold drink, a warm cookie or even letting him crawl back into on the couch or bed to get some relax or rest. Know your spouse best, so think of those things in advance; those things that you know he [or she] would appreciate and finding comforting when he [or she] is a bit under the weather or feeling down, makes our spouses feel very important and our relationship needs to be tended to and nurtured.

Partners who think they can explain why their relationship lacks spacks or intimacy, is as a result of the presence of problems, are surprised to find out that they cannot connect even when the problems have gone away. In a marriage, commitment may be strong, but love, intimacy and deep sharing must be present. However, sadly to say but true, some couples never reach the true knowing, of each other and the ongoing ability to abide in love and grow as individual and as a couple. The scripture reveals to us, the long-term fulfilment as God's design and plan for marriage. This intimacy can only develop and grow, when there are boundaries. This is because boundaries denotes who owns what and has the responsibility.

Sexual interactions that feel upsetting afterwards, such as abusive or controlling dynamic within a relationship can often make its way into the bedroom. Sometimes things feel wrong even in the moment, but other times it's a pattern of feeling uncomfortable after the interaction. Either way, an individual who feels consistently unsettled about on-goings within their sexual realtionship, it's a sign that something is wrong. The scripture says, in Proverbs 5:19 "A loving doe, a graceful deer – may her breasts satisfy you always, may you ever be intoxicated with her love." It is no longer about how long you've been married, there is always room for changes, couples in difficulties can plan dates, trips and romantic evenings at home together with this in mind.

Another obstacle to sex in marriage is pressuring your partner toward unhealthy behaviors, like not respecting your partner's decision or tiredness, these are all ways that controlling individual can try to thwart his [or her] partner's attempts to be a healthier, loving and stronger person, because controlling individual thrive on weakening their partners. The scripture says, in song of Solomon 1:2-4 "May he kiss me with the kisses of his mouth! For your love is better than wine. Your oils have a pleasing fragrance, Your name is *like* purified oil; Therefore the maidens love you. Draw me after you and let us run together! The king has brought me into his chambers."

It is very important that there is no space for controlling attitude between partners so that they could cultivate a flourishing relationship, because sex is simple and the more you have it, the more you want it, so couples must keep their sex life alive and interesting. "Spicing it up" with kindness, gentleness, love and patience. A serious obstacle to sex in marriage and solution is in the research book "Ministry and Community: Recognizing, Healing, and Preventing Ministry Impairment", By Len Sperry. Sexually abusive is the more generic term referring to any instance of sexual violation, while sexual abusing refers to sexual violation that takes place within the area of a professional relationship in which the violation occurs within a sacred trust (Sperry, 2000, 26).[44] Sexual

---

[44] Sperry, Len. Ministry and Community: Recognizing, Healing, and Preventing Ministry Impairment. <u>Liturgical Press</u>, 2000 (p26).

domination involves two adults more often of different rather than of the same gender. Sexually dominating individuals exhibit a recurring pattern of exerting significant control emotional and mental as well as sexual, over another person. The dynamics of mental, emotional, and physical domination are noteworthy in some cases. Violation of sexual boundaries and preying on the emotional vulnerabilities of another are never justifiable. Intervention for this act in a relationship is psychiatric treatment is necessary. In some instance, individual psychotherapy is the first option for both paedophilia and sexual domination. In most instances, it is not an appropriate intervention unless it is a focused psychotherapy that is combined with medication, group therapy, or in-patient or residential treatment. However, there are some different focused therapies worth consideration like, sexual addiction therapy developed by Carnes (1989).

Any individual who betrays the partner by having sex outside of their bonded relationship is faced with reporting it or keeping the secret relationship apart from their home life. The illusion is that reporting this will not break down their primary relationship. The reality is that not only do most secret affairs become exposed, they rupture the trust and in many cases end the relationship. At the very least, they off-set the expected and predicted sense of trust. In many ways, it is a life crisis for both partners. Betrayal leaves everyone feeling like a failure and recovery is only possible if the denial of secrecy is replaced with the honesty of openness.

A healthy sex in marriage, can be cultivated by couples when attracts each other's attention with kidness, gentleness and quality time, whether it's for support, conversation, interest, play, affirmation, feeling connected or for affection, according to relationship coach and therapist, these are moments of opportunity to connect with partner. The scripture says, in Sons of Solomon 4:10 "How delightful is your love, my sister, my bride! How much more pleasing is your love than wine, and the fragrance of your perfume more than any spice" An individual who responds to his [or her] partner by acknowledges them when they are trying to get their attention (although not every attempt will be recognized), but it shows that they are meeting their partner's emotional needs. So couples can increase their awareness of when each person tries to connect with the other to strengthen their relationship.

The truth is, we all want to feel loved and desired by the person we have committed to spend the rest of our life with. Somewhere along the journey, things get in the way; unexpected life and family events. Couples may be physically present together, but it feels like they are miles away. The spark and excitement is starting to wane and slowly growing apart. This lack of intimacy in a marriage can easily lead to frustrations, feeling neglected, resentment, anger, and even divorce. There is no need to despair or give up becsuse no matter how hopeless an individual may feel about the marriage situation, they can rekindle intimacy, sex with the spouse. In some cases couples missing when they first met, deep connection, meaningful conversations, and excitement need to reconnect, grow together and rekindle in the marriage intimancy and sex. This would result in a happier, satisfying, fulfilling and healthier marriage. Couples in this situation must learn or relearn how to connect or reconnect with one another, so that they can rekindle the marriage. Couple must be determined to overcome emotional, physical, and sexual intimacy issues like mismatched sexual desires in the bedroom. Communicate feelings to one another with courage, even feeling hurt, frustration or anger. Couples must learn to deal with anxiety about intimacy for each other's sake and create a safe haven so that they can be vulnerable with each other without feeling judged. Giving attention to daily activities together, has proven to strengthen intimacy, for example deeper conversations, building trust, intellectual and emotional intimacy. A marriage without emotional and sexual intimacy is bound to be unfulfilling. So, couples who want to enhance intimacy in their marriage must rekindle the romance, and have satisfying sex, because emotional and sexual Intimacy in marriage will change the way couples relate with each other.

TWELVE

Controlling Relationship

Controlling relationship is when an individual in a relation manipulates another individual into doing something that is suitable to him [or her], i.e doing what he [or she] wants or desires. This pattern of behaviour can happen in every kind of relationship; for example between friends, among family members, even between colleagues. Being in a controlling relationship greatly but eventually affects, the marriage and a person's life. The fact is, it changes an individual's life completely. Some of the few techniques that a controlling individual uses to mess with the partner's mind are mind games and emotional manipulation, which drains the partner completely, because it makes him [or her] to forget about everything and everyone around, forget self-worth and eventually, lose himself [or herself] completely. An individual in control makes his [or her] partner emotionally dependent on him [or her], by behaviour manipulation in a way, that he [or she] desires.

The couples where one partner is dominant and wants to be always in charge or control, while the other is always silent and agrees with everything the partner does and says. An individual in a controlling relationship, have strong feelings for his [or her] partners and it could become very difficult to break free from that emotional abuse. That kind of toxic relationship leaves indelible marks on children's mental health and their self-esteem. This kind of abusive behaviour can also be found in marriage, where the individual thinks that he [or she] has the right to control the life of his [or her] partner. The spouse want to know where his [or her] partner spend every single minute of the day and text continuously all day, asking about the where about and planned time to be back home and if it happens that no feedback arrived, he [or she] gets angry and accuse the partner of cheating or having another life priority.

The partner is not allowed to do anything without an expressed permission, or at least without discussing it with the controlling partner. An individual who isolates his [or her] partner from other important people like family members, loved ones and friends because his [or her] thinks they represent a threat is living in an unhealthy and manipulative relationship. Such individual may even try to make the partner believe that his [or her] is the only person that can be trusted. It may begin slowly, gently and silently, but this is often the starting point for a controlling and probably manipulative individual's methods. The individual could complain about how often the partner dialogue with a friend on the phone, his [or her] doesn't like the partner's best friend, friends and doesn't think the partner should spend so much time with any particular best friend or friends. Another approach could be an attempt to turn the partner against anyone that his [or her] partner rely on for support. The goal is to strip the partner of any external strength or network support and so become unable to stand up against the controlling individual.

However, in the presence of the partner's loved ones or family members the attitude is completely different, i.e. faking gentleness, kindness and love. An individual who seek desperately to be completely trusted, respected and don't want anyone to suspect the real motives or intentions. An individual who will do anything possible to make his [or her] partner think that the relationship is the only thing that should be important in life simply to create emotional dependency and seeking permission everytime before doing anything. This controlling will eventually lead to the whole aspect of life style and soon enough it will could affect all aspects of the partner's life. It could leads to complete control bringing about loss of connections, lack of new opportunities, and difficulties to achieve personal dreams and goals. This could eventually leads to low self-esteem and lack of confidence. It is so bad that a partner that started such relationship with low self-esteem issues, will still have his [or her] confidence be greatly affected by the controlling partner.

The intention of the controlling individual is to make the partner feel or think that his [or her] is not worthy of being loved and that his [or her] won't find another person to love, if they decide to put an end to the relationship. This great manipulator, will make his [or her] partner become self-worthless "doubting person." Furthermore, such an individual will make the partner to feel guilty, and make his [or her] do whatever, just for the sake of forgiveness and stopping the guilty feelings. In addition the partner must continuously prove his [or her] love to prevent upsetting the controlling partner. An individual can never be relaxed or feel comfortable in such a relationship, because it seems that the controlling individual is waiting for the partner to make a mistake so that he [or she] can use it against the partner and continue with his [or her] tactique of guilt tripping. The partner is afraid to speak up because his [or her] opinion isn't important and as such he [or she] says nothing, which makes the relationship very unhealthy.

A controlling individual must always be consulted, even for some insignificant thing, to prevent anger, and in the event of an error, some foolish mistake, may result is automatic silent treatment. To make the partner work hard to receive forgiveness. A controlling partner typically feels that he [or she] has the right to know more than the actual case. It could be snooping secret or openly demand that the partner must share every details, it is a complete violation of boundaries; checking partner's phone, logs into email, or constantly tracking Internet history, and justifing this actions, It's a complete violation of privacy, this police-like presence within a relationship. Ironically, a controlling individual can show the partner affection, love, and could shower with even compliments when family members and friends are present to camouflage perfect or healthy relationship, but gets angry without any reason. The partner is constantly criticized (toxic habit), by the controlling individual with the intention to impose lack of self-worth and destroy partner's self-esteem.

This individual is so manipulative that will pretends to be the best, making the partner believe to be lucky, having him [or her] in the relationship. Getting into tired arguments to relent, to exert influence, openly argumentative and embrace conflict to control the partner. This controlling individual is likely to triumph in every disagreement that comes up, just because the partner being controlled is more conflict-avoidant in nature or simply exhausted. Every healthy relationship is based on setting boundaries. Manipulative individual knows that setting those boundaries will put a stop from being able to control the partner's life. This individual crosses all boundaries in placed in the relationship, claiming it is done in love.

In marriage, the threats of controlling individual do not have to be physical in nature to be problematic or abusive. But threats of leaving, cutting off certain privileges, even threats harming himself [or herself] can be emotionally manipulative as the threat of physical violence. The partner being controlled could feel stuck in a relationship not out of fear for his [or her] life, but fear of the partner's self-destruct or self-harm in case of separation. An individual may be threatened with losing the home, access to children, and financial support, in the event of breakup or separation from the controlling or abusive partner. The autenticicity of the threats, real, true, fake or genuine, is not the point but another way for the controlling individual to get what he [or she] wants at the expense of the partner. Another cause of controlling behaviour is chronic jealousy of everything and giving of ultimatum. No individual should give an ultimatum, because it is manipulating or threating to accomplish personal desire or self-interest. Controlling partners always give selfish ultimatums to a partner, like threat to end the relationship, if their partner doesn't do as was requested. In fact, giving ultimatums is one of the techniques of a manipulator, because knowing the partner in fear of hurting feelings will accept do whatever is requested.

Unfortunately, most of the cases of a controlling partner in an intimate relationship end with physical abuse, because frequent outbursts of emotions, and controlling partners could eventually become aggressive and violent, if the situation is not addressed. It could start with punishing his [or her] partners every time a mistake is made. The problem is the feelings of the controlled partner, sometimes is too strong and that makes his [or her] to believe that the controlling partner behaviour will eventually change for good. The partner become too emotionally dependent on the controlling partners and too afraid to end the relationship. The partner eventually think that the abuse is normal.

The controlling partner could also control the partner's life because of a fear of abandonment. The love is so much and don't want to ever lose partner, not aware involved in a controlling relationship. An individual who wants to be in charge or control at all times. The need to control the life of the partner is very strong and having a partner with low self-esteem can also make an individual to become even more controlling in marriage. Lack of self-confidence, can trigger so many unpleasant feelings like anxiety, depression, and jealousy, making an individual to become controlling wrongly thinking it's the solution to self-protection, from future bad experience.

In the research book by Luna Parker "Controlling Men - How to cope with and transform your controlling husband or boyfriend." The author makes it clear that first and foremost awareness is the first step in solving any problem. The point here is that it is totally possible to be with a controlling partner, without ever actually realizing it. This will often land the individual in more serious trouble (Parker, 2014)[45]. Recongnizing that there is something wrong with the relationship, and that it is being brought about by the controlling behaviour of the partner, is the first step in coming up with right solution. An individual who is controlling can make the partner feel confused, and suffocated. In marriage, some of the solutions to this problem or abuse are reconnection with close friends and relatives, getting immediate contact with family members, loved ones and close colleagues. The individual should feel free to speak up, everyone must have the

---

[45] Parker, Luna. Controlling-Men:How to cope with and transform your controlling husband or boyfriend. CreateSpace Independent Publishing Platform (September 4, 2014)

right to express personal opinion about everything. Relationships are all about equality and if a partner can't accept this fact, he has problem and should seek counselling immediately. No individual should be afraid to say no (when necessary), and should not be afraid of the partner's reaction, because couples do not have to agree on everything. Boundaries must exist in every healthy relationship, because the main cause of controlling partner's abusive behavior is the lack of boundaries in relationship. The good news is boundaries can be set when not available or reset when broken. Working on self-confidence removes low self-esteem, prevents having a controlling person. No individual should make another feel unworthy. Every individual is created by God almighty or born to be self-worthy and deserve to be loved and treated with respect.

THIRTEEN

Transparency in Relationship
(Avoid too many secrets)

The importance of transparency in a healthy and loving relationship cannot be over emphasied. In a relationship, you definitely want to find someone who likes you for who you are. It's vital "that you can just be you," Dr. Ramani Durvasula, author of "Should I Stay or Should I Go: Surving a Relationship With A Narcissist" You don't want to have to feel like you need to "break a sweat being the 'aspirational avatar'" - you should just be able to show up and be you. An individual should find someone who allows him [or her] to be honest and feel safe doing so. He goes on to say that "If you rush to the bathroom to put your makeup on before he (or she) wakes up because you are afraid of what will happen if he (or she) sees the real you, then you are missing that one thing," Durvasula adds. That is not maintainable long-term (Durvasula, 2017).[46]

There is a delicate balance between privacy and transparency. Privacy is defined as the state or condition of being free from being observed or disturbed by other people. It is the state of being free from public exposure and attention. We all need privacy as individuals and as couples. Psychologically, we understand that whereas secure attachment is key to early development, the growing capacity of the child to internalize this attachment and to separate, to have room to

---

[46] Durvasula, Ramani Should I Stay or Should I Go: Surving a Relationship With A Narcissist. Post Hill Press; Reprint edition (October 24, 2017).

be, to play alone, to have private thoughts, to have space, to develop an authentic self is crucial. In relationship we need different degrees of privacy to re-charge, regulate stress and nurture a sense of self, be it a solitary hobby or reading the paper alone.

However, we all need intimacy, to be and share with another, to be known by someone in a way that no one else knows us. This intimacy must be accompined with transparency. In every relationship we need transparency, or better still transparency is a necessity, very essential and very important. In the life of a couple it signifies honesty, frankness, truth and loyalthy in the interaction between spouses. Transparency help to maintain unity, love and peace within the relationship. An individual that explain clearly details of his action to his [or her] spouse brings in trust and faith in the relationship, because informing the spouse about all decision or activities is an easy thing which delivers great result, unity and onness in marriage.

There are certain areas that lack of transparency has caused great damage in relationship, for example lack of transparency in dealing with money, have led to marriage failure and divorce. An individual have the right to help his [or her] family members or better still the parents, with part of the hard earned income, that is not the issue, the point is there is no need or right to hide it from the partner. Couples should be free to openly discuss with the partner every financial responsibility or assistance towards family members in general and parents in particular. In a healthy relationship the spouse must not refuse when this done transparently or openly. Another issue that is equally important for the sake of transparency, is extra-marital friendship, spouse should not have questionable or suspicious friendship with a colleague or friend without the knowledge of the partner.

Privacy is fine, essential and in my consideration everyone should have privacy but not secrecy. Privicy is space for an individual and the spouse, because they are both different person with diverse wishes and desires. The private needs of an individual to fulfil his [or her] own personal wishes should be respected by both parties within the relationship. In counselling, I always suggest that spouses should sit down and have a very candid discussion, together instead of each spouse making their your own decision without informing one another. There shouldn't be any space for any form of secrecy in the behaviour of spouses towards one another. When there is secrecy, spouses tend to hide everything about themselves from one another which lead to a deep sense of insecurity, anxiety, distrust, boring and tedious relationship.

The solution is always boundaries, that is "give enough freedom to your spouse and you will get you freedom." This is not freedom to do as you wish but to discuss, inform and explain to your spouse details about your affairs without secrecy. In a healthy relationship, marriage should be redreshing, energizing and must have as the "water of life" crystal clear transparency or else it won't be full of "life and love". There are various indications to identify in couples when this "life and love" or transparency is lacking in a relationship. When a spouse is persistently late from work without giving valid reason or informing the partner, an individual not informing the partner about any financial dealing and taking calls in another room on mobile to avoid the partner listening to the conversation. However, we all need boundaries and boundaries changes in relationship, So in a committed and intimate relationship, our individual boundaries of privacy must change.

In marriage, we choose to share the best and worst of ourselves, confidences, money, vacations, hardship, fears, bedrooms and sex with another individual. In addition we also share a respect for each other's privacy and so a loving relationship has room for two independent people as well as their mutual dependency. It is a secret and not private, if an individual decides to hide an online relationship with a former high school sweetheart or withholding the loss of family money due to gambling or a business investment. There is evidence that secrets can be motivated by betrayal, shame, fear, or anger and very act disqualify intimacy because it prevents authenticity. Psychologically, in marriage when a partner is holding a secret, a part of them is not available for connection with the spouse.

On the other hand, when privacy is lacking, without separate space, romance wanes, as there is no room for imagination. It is difficult to fantasize about someone standing next to us, most of the time. When there is no privacy " to be oneself" in a relationship, partners conform to expectations, which makes authenticity and creativity almost impossible. However, when individuals are allowed to have private dreams, they very often become shared possibilities, although one partner may be more disclosing than the other. In a trusting relationship, there is no need to check each other's phone, emails, mail or spy on daily moves, nor the obligation to disclose it all. When ever couples enjoy sharing, it is always mutual sharing that links, binds and bring greater unity in connection. The danger is, when there is conscious motivation to keep something unknown or hide something that directly impacts a partner and the bond is not shared, privacy becomes secrecy.

I would suggest that before any individual discloses personal details to the partner, he [or she] most firstly examine the purpose of that disclosure; disclosing for the sake of greater intimacy or as a confession for your own benefit; will it help or hurt the other person and will transparency lead to greater trust, empathy, or simply to suspicion and distrust; However, if the goal is greater intimacy and true love, it can't be built on what an individual wants the partner to see, but the person he [or she] really is or true-self, so be "real." Transparency in Relationship grows then as we become more aware that, in our experience, God is trusthworthy, and as we become better able to express our own deeper attitudes (Barry, 2009, 40).[47] The more experience an individual have in prayer, the more likely he [or she] will let more than thought enter our prayer, because he [or she] will spontaneously seek ways of expressing himself [or herself] more fully. Ascetical practises such as fasting allow the body to express attitude, and so enable the person to enter more fully into communication with God.

---

[47] Barry, W.A., Connally, W.J. The Practice ofSpiritual Direction. HarperOne; 2nd Revised ed. edition (June 2, 2009) P40.

FOURTEEN

Adoption of Prayer

What a privilege to communicate with the creator of heaven and earth, The Almighty God. The secret ingredient to a healthy relationship and most especially to a happy marriage is not love but prayer. Prayer is a powerful tool, the essential ingredient needed in our lives which not only enable us to speak directly to God, but prayer allows God to talk to us about our relationships with other people. Through prayer, God can lead us to initiate new relationships, provide unique opportunities to grow current relationships and even provide wisdom in how to best approach awkward, difficult relationships. Constant, daily prayer with God provides insight into so many facets of our lives and should not be focused solely on our relationships with other people because God can provide help, and answers to, an infinite number of concerns and trials. Adoption of Prayer is so important in a relationship because it helps us to understand what God's desire is for our lives, individually and as a married couple.

Moreover, it also helps the marriage couple to understand their purpose and why they live for Christ. The good thing about prayer, is that God is never too busy, distracted or impatient but always willing to listen to our achievements, requests, questions and fears. God is never indifferent or complains that a concern is too big or too small for his attention. God has time for anything and everything. The scriptures says in Hebrew 10:23 "Let us hold unswervingly to the hope we profess, for he who promised is faithful." In addition, prayer gives God the opportunity to let his voice be heard and essentially a conversation between you and God, gives direction and meaning to life. This conversation is not one-sided because God wants to be heard as well as spoken to, and He wants a chance to speak truthfully about what he thinks about life. God wants to share with us what His plans, desire and purpose for life and longs always to provide us with the needed wisdom and direction. God in His words, also wants to align our life to coincide with His ultimate plan and purpose.

Some individuals may not consider a relationship with God as a vital part of their life and do not seek out conversation with God on a daily basis, like they would seek out fellowship with a friend. These individuals fail to recognize that God exists and wants to have a relationship with everyone, just like the relationship between a father and his child. It seems rather simple to understand because it is a step in the right direction, ways to incorporate fresh perspective in the relationship and creating that special connection that comes from time spent daily in study, prayer and meditation.

In the research study of a book, "High Definition Life Going Throttle - For Life's Best by Luis Palau, he writes "of course, there's praying and then there's praying. As a young man I used to attend a weekly all-night prayer meeting with friends. But typically I prayed with a negative attitude towards life. I would wake up in the morning and spend time reading the Bible, but my prayer always sounded like weeping and crying rather than joy and exuberance in the Holy Spirit. Then when I was about twenty-six years old, my wife and I participated in a seven-month missionary internship program. One day the instructor asked, "How do you start your day with the Lord? Do you get up and say, 'What a day, here we go again! Now goes the alarm. It always seems to ring too early. It's Monday and I have to go to work again. Somebody, please help me make it to the five o'clock news. Do you start with a snivelling and a pleading prayer? Or do you start with a note of praise and glory to God? His word struck home. I began to notice that positive believers such as apostle Paul aleways began with a note of optimism and expectation: The scripture says, in 2 Corinthians 2:14, "But thanks be to God, who always leads us as captives in Christ's triumphal procession and uses us to spread the aroma of the knowledge of him everywhere." "Now wherever we go God uses us to tell others about the Lord and to spread the Good News like a sweet perfume" (Palau, 2005,46,48,49).[48] What a powerful testimony, about how a different approach to 'The Word of God' and prayer can change our life and help foster relationship between God and others.

In a healthy relationship couples who can comfortably share downtime without words, without a task to perform and even without the need to interact and relate in mutual meditation, is a good sign that both can stand together on life's unpredictable journey. Partners who can learn to experience silence together without feeling worried that something is wrong is a good test of compatibility. Couples should take meditation as a tool that enables relationship health and success, although it can be tempting to spend all day weekends together, it's important to have separate work lives and spend some time apart from time to time. Taking time for ourselves may seem selfish, as though we're avoiding our partner, but in fact, brief periods of meditation recharge our soul batteries, allow us to give even more to our partners, to the relationship itself and have a secure attachment with each other.

When it comes to marriage, all of us live in a hurricane zone. And since the pressures, crises, and tragedies of life seldom blow in without advance warning, it is during the calm stretches of life that we must get ready for them. Persevering love is founded on the devotion and friendship a husband and wife build before the storm strikes. Work on a Bible study together. Take a second honeymoon. Read some good books on marriage enrichment and discuss them together. Attend a Christian marriage conference. Seek out a biblically based Christian counsellor, and ask him [or her] for pointers on how to deepen your friendship.

---

[48] Palau, Luis, High Definition Life Going Throttle - For Life's Best; Fleming H Revell Co (March 1, 2005) P46-49.

The scripture declares, in Proverbs 14:1 "A wise woman builds her home, but a foolish woman tears it down with her own hands." Spouses who pray daily are making marriage a higher priority, while those who fail to realize the importance of prayer are struck in the event of a problem to discover how life can change in a matter of seconds. The reality is, married couples should find the time to honour one another, share intimacy and spending time together in prayer becomes extremely important in keeping the relationship a priority. Couples should have this goal in mind, taking the time to make prayer a priority in their calendar, so that no one will mistakenly give to the other what they need rather than what he [or she] needs. Pray for your spouse, ask him [or her] what you can pray for him [or her] in particular that day.

Take time to give each other encouragement and praise for an area that both especially appreciate. If a partner is having a rough day, take the time to encourage him [or her] with kind words. Couples must desire to have a deeper and more fulfilling relationship together in prayer and daily devotional could help to make it easier to read and simple to follow. Through prayers, we develop our belief in God and His Son Jesus Christ and it the reason, Apostle Paul encouraged Christians to pray in the Spirit (Jude 20). Jesus set an example for the Christians by praying so frequently that His disciples requested Him to educate them on how to pray. Prayer will strengthen the believer, marriage, family, relationship and build up bravery in Christ, with confidence in God to perform the impossible.

However, prayer is actually a two-way channel through which God and human beings communicate with one another. Communication is extremely important for any relationship on this planet. By means of prayers, Christians relate their feelings, minds, emotions, needs and inadequacies, whilst God communicates solutions, assurance and also His superiority to the believers. God is love and by prayers, an individual can experience and comprehend more of the love of Christ. The scripture says in Ephesians 4:15 "Instead, speaking the truth in love, we will grow to become in every respect the mature body of him who is the head, that is, Christ." Whenever an individual prays, he [or she] enters into the presence of God and surrounded by God's grace, mercy and love. This guantees the couples protection of God, insecurity fades away and the result is courage to deal with life realizing that Christ loves and Presence.

In a healthy relationship, couples pray, ask and receive their request or needs from God. The Lord Jesus instrusted everyone to ask, if we wish to receive from the Almighty God. The scripture in James 4:2 says, "You desire but do not have, so you kill. You covet but you cannot get what you want, so you quarrel and fight. You do not have because you do not ask God." James stated that we don't have simply because we haven't asked. Consequently, whatever an individual or a couple desires from the Almighty God should requested or presented in prayer prior to receiving it. Christians marriages triumph over Satan, difficulties, hard times, good times, opposition, oppression, etc... through prayers. Satan the adversary has been conquered by the death and the resurrection of the Lord Jesus Christ, but individuals or couples must implement it through prayers in the name of Christ. As it is stated, "a prayerless Christian is actually a powerless Christian". While you pray, you implement your authority in Jesus against all the assaults of the foe or enemy.

I would like to conclude quoting this research study book [49]"Since You Asked by Don Gossett, There is great strentgth in the united prayers of two believers (couples). The scripture says, in Matthew 18:19, "Again, truly I tell you that if two of you on earth agree about anything they ask for, it will be done for them by my Father in heaven." Have an agreement-partner with whom you can share your prayer burdens. Pray according to the pattern our Lord Jesus, set forth, praying to the Father in the name of Jesus.".... The scripture says in John 15:16, You did not choose me, but I chose you and appointed you so that you might go and bear fruit-fruit that will last- and so that whatever you ask in my name the Father will give you."

It is important that we follow the scriptural pattern and pray, not to Jesus, but to the Father in the blessed name of our Lord and

---

[49] Gossett, Don, Since You Asked; Whitaker House. 1979.

Saviour Jesus Christ. We are then positively assured of great answers! Pray for everything! The scripture says in Philippians 4:6, "Do not be anxious about anything, but in every situation, by prayer and petition, with thanksgiving, present your requests to God." Dare to ask God for miracles. God wants to give his family more than that which they can barely need to squeak by this life. God wants to give couples their heart's desire. God as promised is faithful and the adoption of Prayer in marriage, by couples who have faith and believe, will enable them to receive answers to their prayers and even some times when they don't receive will still be full of joy and peace.

I would like to conclude with the suggestion on page 88 'Flowing As One-Flesh In The Gift' from the research study book [50]"Married for life - Life giving principles that make a marriage last by marriage ministries." – Become sensitive as to how He (God) would use the two of you togrther (couple); When one spouse operates in a gift the other often is a confirmation; As you spend time in prayer together, expect the Holy Spirit to flow through you as one-flesh in the gift; The gifts are not reserved for "special" people, sign and wonders follow all who believe; Teach your children about Spiritual gifts; Finally, develop your prayer life and be amazed at the way the Holy Spirit will move through you.

---

[50] Married for life - Life giving principles that make a marriage last by marriage ministries international ISDN 1-884794-02-5 (P88).

CONCLUSION

Finally, we all know that life is made up of different types of relationship and an individual level of satisfaction and success is determined by what he [or she] does, how he [or she] does it, and what he [or she] represents. This research study shows that the proper adoption of the various factors illustrated in this document in the correct manner will result in a fulfilling and healthy relationship. This research has dealt with issues and provided practical solutions to various mistakes, that are unhealthy for couples to dwell in which result in unfulfilling relationship. The thing that makes this research so exciting and ground-breaking is looking at relationship in terms of "Adopting Measures and Approaches to Ensure Healthy Relationship" has provided concrete suggestions for ways couples can deepen and enrich connection as individuals and as partners, to live out their years together.

There may be a period when couples do not feel all that happy, or even all that satisfied, but couples should know that in the long run, adopting these measures and approaches they will be satisfied and fulfilled. Relationships are hard work and for an individual to be "always perfect" at loving his [or her] partner does not always come too easy to every couple. However, to believers (in particular) the love of God has being shed in our heart by the Holy Ghost, so we can love with the God kind of love without pre-conditions, but to everyone (in general), i.e. to everyone in whatever kind of relationship and definitely for couples, this research study has provided proven measures and skill that can and must be learnt and practice to ensure a healthy and fulfilling relationship.. These measures and approaches indicated in this document can be studied and the research can be applied to improve and promote healthy couple's relationship. This study research has revealed that although relationships could have problems and conflicts because couples have different perceptions and react differently in addressing or confronting issues, there is always a common ground to solution and happy relationship. Relationship issues are common in every home because of different exposure and lifestyles and even Christian's homes struggle with issues, that cannot be neglected but dealt with effectively using psychological, sociological, and biblical principles. That is exactly what this research study has done providing practical adoptable measures and approaches to the key factor which is the ability for couples to live together in love and trust; and also suggesting solutions and ways couples could use their disagreements to stimulate growth, develop their lives, maintain happy and healthy relationship.

BIBLIOGRAPHY
WITH REFERENCES

1. Baker, Don. *Beyond Forgiveness: The Healing Touch of Church Discipline*. Portland, Or.: Multnomah Press, 1984.
2. Barry, William A., and William J. Connolly. *The Practice of Spiritual Direction*. New York: HarperOne, 2009.
3. Chapman, Gary D., and Amy Summers. *The Five Love Languages: How to Express Heartfelt Commitment to Your Mate*. Nashville, TN: LifeWay Press, 2016.
4. Cloud, Henry, and John Sims Townsend. *Boundaries in Marriage*. Grand Rapids: Zondervan, 1999.
5. Durvasula, Ramani. *Should I Stay or Should I Go?: Surviving a Relationship with a Narcissist*. New York, NY: Post Hill Press, 2017.
6. Evans, Jimmy. *Marriage on the Rock: Gods Design for Your Dream Marriage*. Amarillo, TX: Majestic Media, 2012.
7. Evans, Jimmy, and Craig Groeschel. *The Four Laws of Love: Guaranteed Success for Every Married Couple*. Dallas, TX: XO Publishing, 2019.
8. Gosett, Don. *Since You Asked--*. Springdale, PA: Whitaker House, 1979.
9. Graham, Billy. *The Key to Personal Peace*. W. Publishing Group., 2005.
10. Graham, Billy. *Peace with God: The Secret of Happiness*. Nashville, TN: W Publishing Group, an Imprint of Thomas Nelson, 2017.

11. Graham, Billy. *The Inspiration Writings: Peace with God - The Secret of Happiness - Answers to Life's Problems*. New York: Inspirational Press, 1995.

12. Linn, Matthew, and Dennis Linn. *Healing of Memories*. New York: Paulist Press, 1974.

13. Lowe, Janet. *Billy Graham Speaks: insight into the world's greatest preacher*. New York, NY: John Wiley, 1999

14. Mains, David R. *Healing the Dysfunctional Church Family: When Destructive Family Patterns Infiltrate the Body of Christ*. Shippensburg, PA: Destiny Image Publishers, 1995.

15. Osteen, Joel. *Break Out!: 5 Keys to Go beyond Your Barriers and Live an Extraordinary Life*. New York: FaithWords, 2014.

16. Osteen, Joel. *Your Best Life Now: 7 Steps to Living at Your Full Potential*. New York: FaithWords, 2015.

17. Osteen, Joel. *Become a Better You: 7 Keys to Improving Your Life Every Day*. New York: Howard Books, 2017.

18. Palau, Luis, and Steve Halliday. *High Definition Life: Going Full Throttle for Lifes Best*. Grand Rapids, MI: Fleming H. Revell, 2005.

19. Palau, Luis, and Steve Halliday. *High Definition Life: Trading Lifes Good for Gods Best*. Grand Rapids, MI: Revell, 2005.

20. Parker, Luna. Controlling Men: How to cope with and transform your controlling husband or boyfriend. CreateSpace Independent Publishing Platform, September 4, 2014

21. Parsley, Rod. *He Came First: Following Christ to Spiritual Breakthrough*. Nashville: T. Nelson Publishers, 2002.

22. Phillips, Mike. *Married for Life: Life-giving Principles That Make a Marriage Last: Leadership Manual*. Littleton, CO: Eden Pub., 2000.

23. Rosenberg, Marshall B. *Nonviolent Communication: A Language of Life*. Encinitas: Puddledancer Press, 2015.

24. Sperry, Len. *Ministry and Community: Recognizing, Healing, and Preventing Ministry Impairment*. Collegeville, MN: Liturgical Press, 2000.

25. Stanley, Charles F. *Living the Extraordinary Life: Nine Principles to Discover It.* Nashville: Nelson Books, 2005.

26. Seven-Principles-For-Making-Marriage-Work:https://www.gottman.com/product/the-seven-principles-for-making-marriage-work/#&gid=1&pid=2

27. Scripture quotations are from the Holy Bible - New International Version, https://biblehub.com/ New American Standard Bible Copyright © 1960, 1962, 1963, 1968, 1971, 1972, 1973, 1975, 1977, 1995 by The Lockman Foundation, La Habra, Calif. All rights reserved. For Permission to Quote Information visit http://www.lockman.org

28. https://positivepsychology.com/

29. https://journals.sagepub.com/doi/full/10.1177/2374373517699267

30. https://yourlifepathco.com/

31. https://whww.journal33.org/index.html

32. http://ihd.berkeley.edu/research-centers/greater-good-science-center

33. https://blog.prepare-enrich.com/2018/02/5-ways-to-celebrate-your-relationship/

34. Eight-Dates: https://www.gottman.com/eight-dates/

35. © Decision Magazine, July 2010

THANK YOU!

I'd like to use this time to thank you for purchasing my books and helping my ministry and work.

You have already accomplished so much, but I would appreciate an honest review of some of my books on your favorite retailer. This is critical since reviews reflect how much an author's work is respected.

Please be aware that I read and value all comments and reviews. You can always post a review even though you haven't finished the book yet, and then edit your reviews later.

Thank you so much as you spare a precious moment of your time and may God bless you and meet you at the very point of your need.

Please send me an email at dr.pastormanny@gmail.com if you encounter any difficulty in leaving your review.

You can also send me an email at dr.pastormanny@gmail.com if you need prayers or counsel or you have questions. Better still if you want to be friends with me.

OTHER BOOKS BY EMMANUEL ATOE

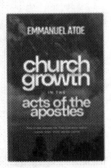

Church Growth in the Acts of the Apostles

The Church is the most powerful corporate body that is capable of commanding the attention of heaven on earth. The Church is God's idea and product, and so possesses an inbuilt capacity for success. The objective of this book is to get you acquainted with the purpose of the church in general, and the vision of Victory Sanctuary in particular.

A Moment of Prayer

There is nothing impossible with God but praying while breaking the law of God makes your prayers ineffective. Therefore, in this book, A Moment of Prayer, everyone under this program is expected to pray according to the rule, not against the law supporting it.

The Believer's Handbook

This book is highly recommendable for all. It is a book that will enhance your spiritual life, ignite the fire in you. It is a book that will open your heart to the mystery of faith.

The inestimable value of this book to every soul cannot be over emphasized. With this book you will get to know about the pillars of true faith in God. If you have been doubting your salvation, Christian life, the person and baptism of the Holy Ghost etc., this book is all you need.

Printed in the United States
by Baker & Taylor Publisher Services